Thinking Musically

∞

EXPERIENCING MUSIC, EXPRESSING CULTURE

∞

BONNIE C. WADE

New York   Oxford
Oxford University Press
2004

Oxford University Press

Oxford   New York
Auckland   Bangkok   Buenos Aires   Cape Town   Chennai
Dar es Salaam   Delhi   Hong Kong   Istanbul   Karachi   Kolkata
Kuala Lumpur   Madrid   Melbourne   Mexico City   Mumbai
Nairobi   São Paulo   Shanghai   Taipei   Tokyo   Toronto

Copyright © 2004 by Oxford University Press, Inc.

Published by Oxford University Press, Inc.
198 Madison Avenue, New York, New York, 10016
http://www.oup-usa.org

Oxford is a registered trademark of Oxford University Press

Library of Congress Cataloging-in-Publication Data
Wade, Bonnie C.
   Thinking musically : experiencing music, expressing culture / by Bonnie C. Wade.
      p. cm.—(Global music series)
   Includes bibliographical references (p.) and index.
   Contents: Thinking about music—Thinking about instruments—Thinking about
time—Thinking about pitch—Thinking about structure—Thinking about issues—
Thinking about fieldwork.
   ISBN-13: 978-0-19-513664-7
   ISBN-10: 0-19-513664-0 (pbk. : alk. paper)—ISBN 0-19-513663-2 (cloth : alk. paper)
      1. Ethnomusicology. I. Title. II. Series.

ML3798.W33 2003
780'.8—dc21

                                                                    2003041940

Printing number: 9 8 7 6

Printed in the United States of America
on acid-free paper

Thinking Musically

Contents

∞

Foreword

∞

In the past three decades interest in music around the world has surged, as evidenced in the proliferation of courses at the college level, the burgeoning "world music" market in the recording business, and the extent to which musical performance is evoked as a lure in the international tourist industry. This heightened interest has encouraged an explosion in ethnomusicological research and publication, including the production of reference works and textbooks. The original model for the "world music" course—if this is Tuesday, this must be Japan—has grown old, as has the format of textbooks for it, either a series of articles in single multiauthored volumes that subscribe to the idea of "a survey" and have created a canon of cultures for study, or single-authored studies purporting to cover world musics or ethnomusicology. The time has come for a change.

This Global Music Series offers a new paradigm. Teachers can now design their own courses; choosing from a set of case study volumes, they can decide which and how many musics they will cover. The series also does something else; rather than uniformly taking a large region and giving superficial examples from several different countries within it, in some case studies authors have focused on a specific culture or a few countries within a larger region. Its length and approach permits each volume greater depth than the usual survey. Themes significant in each volume guide the choice of music that is discussed. The contemporary musical situation is the point of departure in all the volumes, with historical information and traditions covered as they elucidate the present. In addition, a set of unifying topics such as gender, globalization, and authenticity occur throughout the series. These are addressed in the framing volume, *Thinking Musically*, which sets the stage for the case studies by introducing ways to think about how people make music meaningful and useful in their lives and presenting basic musical concepts as they are practiced in musical systems around the world. A second framing volume, *Teaching Music Globally*, guides teachers in the use of *Thinking Musically* and the case studies.

The series subtitle, "Experiencing Music, Expressing Culture," also puts in the forefront the people who make music or in some other way experience it and also through it express shared culture. This resonance with global history studies, with their focus on processes and themes that permit cross-study, occasions the title of this Global Music Series.

Bonnie C. Wade
Patricia Shehan Campbell
General Editors

Preface

∞

This book is written to frame and complement a series of case study volumes in the Global Music Series. Whereas each case study focuses on a specific culture or one designated part of the world, this text offers a basis for the contrast and comparison of diverse musics. Whereas each case study is conceived around themes that are significant in its one area, this book speaks to a set of unifying topics that recur in multiple case studies. Whereas authors of the case studies naturally present their material from ethnomusicological perspectives, this volume addresses the field of ethnomusicology more explicitly.

Comparing is not an intellectual exercise I have cared much for, but as a teacher I know that it is inevitable when diverse materials are presented in a course. My task, then, was to find a way to lay the foundation for careful comparison without actually doing it much myself. In deciding how to lay that foundation in this book, there was another major consideration. As co-general editor of the series, I established a guideline for authors that they were not to spend precious pages introducing basic elements of music; their aim was to provide depth in their particular subject. Yet basic elements need to be explained; therefore, while laying a foundation for comparison, I also took on that task.

How was I to do it? Organization by genre (as in Japanese music study), by historical periods (as in study of the European tradition), or by issues (the purview of the case studies in the series) would not make much sense. Turning to my experience of studying North Indian music, I remembered that my teachers initially focused on *rāga* (melody), and one of the first things I had to do was learn how to play the drone ("harmony") and simultaneously sing melody. Then came a focus on *tāla* ("rhythm"), and I was taught to sing in a *rāga* according to a certain formal structure. That experience resonated with the established order of presentation of Western-style music scholarship, and I first drafted the book on that model. Reflecting on my teaching experience in the course of shaping and reshaping the book, I kept returning to the realization that through the years most nonspecialist students actually relate much more easily to rhythm than to discussions of melody and harmony. A reader of the manuscript for Oxford University Press affirmed this and thus liberated me; I decided to break the mold. Each of the basic ingredients of music is indeed discussed in turn, but rhythm comes first. In chapters 3 and 4 I examine the organization of time and then of pitch (both melodically and harmonically), exploring ways they have been conceived and used in the creative musical imaginations of music makers around the globe. This is not a study of repertoire; it is a study of ideas and practices. Likewise, in chapter 5 I examine the structuring of musical selections. Most examples, but not all, are coordinated with the case studies. While the variety of music in the examples may seem bewildering at first, many of them are considered several times in this volume so that they become very familiar.

Topics that unify the case studies are interwoven throughout the book. Consideration of the teaching and learning of music comes in chapter 1. In chapter 2 I present numerous ways of thinking about musical instruments and in chapter 6 speak to issues that are lively in the field of ethnomusicology and that recur in multiple case studies.

With music, the focus that is the most significant in ethnomusicology is people. People make music what it is, and *people make music meaningful and useful in their lives.* That last statement encapsulates much of what ethnomusicologists are interested in, and I offer it as a framing perspective throughout the book for ways of thinking about music. The most distinctive method of ethnomusicological research—learning about music from people—is the subject of chapter 7, a practical guide to students for doing field research on their own.

I must offer a few caveats. In this volume I have scarcely used three terms with which scholars are grappling: "culture," and its extensions, "a culture," and "a music culture" (see chapter 6). The concept of "culture" resulted when modern European nation-states were emerging, bounded and distinctive. The struggle for recognition by a nation-state causes a rhetoric to develop that defines cultural and historical substance or attributes upon which national existence can be said to rest. Thus the idea of "a culture" emerges—something "authentic" that exists only with "a nation." Recently, however, studies of modernization, with its attendant Westernization, and of globalization, with its flow of people, ideas, and goods around the earth, have problematized that bounded concept of "a culture." More generically, social scientists have used the word "culture" to refer to ideas (values, worldview, concepts) and beliefs of individuals and groups of people as well as practices that emerge from those ideas and beliefs. That sense of "culture" is complemented by the term "society," that is, the systems (kinship, political, economic, etc.) that people construct to manage relationships among themselves. Conflating those different senses, common vernacular usage of "a culture" is likely to refer to the society—that is, the social group or social system—with which the cultural set of ideas, beliefs, and practices are associated. In the few instances where I cautiously use the contested term "music culture," I mean the ways in which people make music meaningful and useful in their lives—the ideas, beliefs, practices, and also the systems in evidence in the sphere of music.

Another extension of the idea of "culture" is the "culture area." Beyond the nation-state, large geographical areas of the world, such as Southeast Asia, have been clustered for political reasons, mostly, and scholars, including ethnomusicologists, have also thought in terms of region. In this book I refer to musical areas carefully and seldom. As we learn more about musics on the planet we are less inclined to feel comfortable with the level of generalization they imply.

A final caveat concerns the rubric of "Western music." It is problematic on several counts. The term "Western music" is all too often invoked when reference is intended to refer specifically to music of or derived from European classical musical practices. The term "Western music" is also problematic when viewed from the perspectives of modernization, colonization, and globalization. Resulting from serious enculturation for more than a century, many peoples around the world consume and create music that is still referred to as "Western music" although it is now arguably just as much theirs as "the West's." "The West" is, on the one hand, a concept and, on the other, a geographical location. In this book I use the term "Western music" carefully, preferring a greater degree of specificity.

In the following pages I speak to a number of musical ideas and practices from around the world. In addition to helping you enjoy many kinds of music, I hope that this book will help you to think musically.

ACKNOWLEDGMENTS

This Global Music Series began as a partnership with myself, Patricia Campbell, and then-Oxford University Press music editor Maribeth Payne. I want to acknowledge here the years of stewardship and support by Payne to help the project come to fruition. I thank Campbell as well for being such a good colleague in this large and complex endeavor and for her volume, *Teaching Music Globally*.

This book, *Thinking Musically*, is the most difficult project I have ever undertaken. I could not have written it without the help of many people, too numerous to mention here. Several of them are noted in the figure and CD credits. I want particularly to acknowledge the teamwork and help of my companion authors in the Global Music Series: Matthew Allen and T. Viswanathan (South India), Greg Barz (East Africa), Benjamin Brinner (Java), Shannon Dudley (Trinidad), Lisa Gold (Bali), Scott Marcus (Middle East), Adelaida Reyes (United States), Timothy Rice (Bulgaria), George Ruckert (North India), Stanley Scott and Dorothea Hast (Ireland), Daniel Sheehy (Mexico/Mexican-American), Ruth Stone (West Africa), Lawrence Witzleben (China) and John Murphy (Brazil). Dave Brubeck's personal attention to my remarks about his music and Fred Lerdahl's response to the chapter on time are greatly appreciated. Special thanks also to colleagues Jocelyne Guilbault, for her helpful suggestions on chapter 6, to Karen Rozenak for her encouragement of such a volume and her thoughtful reading of an early draft, Benjamin Brinner and Eliot Bates for their help with the CD and Joseph Dale for Figure 1.12. Cathy Carapella of Diamond Time was most helpful in sorting out the byzantine details of the permission process. And I appreciate the help of Department of Music staff member James Coates with the numerous details involved in those permissions. I also thank the anonymous readers of this manuscript in its various incarnations for their insightful comments and helpful suggestions. And special thanks also go to Jan Beatty, Talia Krohn, Lisa Grzan, and Ellen Welch at Oxford University Press.

Last, but not least, I thank the students in my freshman seminar *Thinking Musically* (spring 2001) at the University of California, Berkeley, for their critical reading of a very early draft, their considered suggestions, assistance with compiling the CD, and other creative efforts, some of which are credited individually in the text: Vicky Bertics, Lyndsy Brown, Shanesha Brooks, Rachelle Callenback, Jane Chiu, Lucia Comnes, Brendan Grady, Pamela Han, Jill Kronick, Lisa McCabe, Johnny Mac, Leslie Mosley, Huy Nguyen, Viet Nguyen, Anna Phan, Tamina Spurney, Janice Tan, and Phuoc Truong.

CD Track List

∞

1 Second *sura* of the Koran, *al-Bagara* (Islamic recitation). Ceremony of the Qadiriya Sufi brotherhood, Mevlevi Sufi, Turkey. *Archives internationales de musique populaire (Musée d'ethnographie, Geneva, 1988).*

2 "Gunslingers" (Trinidadian steelband). *The Steel Drums of Kim Loy Wong.* From *University Settlement Steel Band,* ed. Pete Seeger (Folkways, 1961).

3 "Partridges Flying" (Chinese ensemble). China Records (Zhongguo Changpian, n.d.).

4 "Mi bajo y yo" (*salsa*). Oscar d'Leon, bandleader. From *Exitos y Algo mas* Company, n.d.

5 *Atsiagbeko* (Ghanaian narrative dance). West Africa drum ensemble. Recording and notes by Richard Hill, n.d. Courtesy of Lyrichord Discs.

6 "All for Freedom"; "Calypso Freedom" (American protest song). Sweet Honey in the Rock. From *On to Mississippi* (Music for Little People, c. 1989).

7 "The Ballad of César Chávez" (*corrido*). Pablo and Juanita Saludado. From *Las Voces de los Campesinos,* n.d. Courtesy of the Center for the Study of Comparative Folklore and Mythology, UCLA.

8 "Ketawang Puspawarna" (Javanese *slendro,* pentatonic). Istana Mangkunegaran. From *Javanese Court Gamelan,* vol. 2, c. 1977. Courtesy of Nonesuch Records.

9 Navajo corn-grinding song. Joe Lee, lead singer. Recorded in Lukachukai, Arizona, 17 August 1940, by Laura Boulton. From *Navajo Songs* (Smithsonian Folkways, 1992).

10 "Vikrit recitation." From *The Four Vedas: The Oral Tradition of Hymns, Chants, Sacrificial and Magical Formulas* (Folkways 01426, c. 1968). Courtesy of Smithsonian Folkways Recordings. Used by permission.

11 "Raga Purvi-Kalyan" (North Indian *sitar*). Pandit Ravi Shankar. Ocora Records, 1995.

12 "First Wine Offering: A-ak" (Chinese Confucian music in Korea). Confucian ritual ensemble. Orchestra of the National Music Institute, Seoul, Korea, Kim Ki-su, director. Recorded by John Levy. Lyrichord Discs, 1969.

13 Didjeridu (aboriginal aerophone). A selection from northwestern Australia/Arnhem Land, performed by an unidentified blower (or "puller," as they are called). From *Tribal Music of Australia* (New York: Ethnic Folkways Album P 439, c. 1953).

14 "Conch call" (Tibetan Buddhist ritual). Conch. From *Musique rituelle tibetaine* (Ocora Records OCR 49, [1970]).

15 "Hifumi no Shirabe Hachigaeshi" (Zen Buddhist music). Goro Yamaguchi, *shakuhachi*. Japan Victor, n.d.

16 "Festival Music" (offstage (*geza*) ensemble). From *Music from the Kabuki*. Nonesuch H-72012, [1970].

17 Korean *Komungo Sanjo: Chinyango, Chungmori, Onmori*. Han Kapdeuk, *komungo*; Hwang Deuk-ju, *chang-gu*. Recording offered by the National Center for Korean Traditional Performing Arts, Seoul.

18 "Travelling in Soochow" (Chinese folk instrumental music). Chinese *di-tze* (flute). China Records, n.d.

19 "Kiembara xylophone orchestra," Famankaha, Sous-Prefecture of Korhogo, Ivory Coast, West Africa. From *The Music of the Senufo*. Bärenreiter, UNESCO Collection. *Anthology of African Music*, vol. 8, n.d.

20 Cantonese opera (Chinese vocal, Cantonese style). Fung Hang Record Ltd. (Hong Kong, n.d.).

21 Georges Bizet, "L'amour est un oiseau rebelle" (Habanera) from *Carmen*. Robert Shaw Chorale and Children's Chorus from l'Elysée Francaise. Robert Shaw, Conductor. Fritz Reiner conducting the RCA Victor Orchestra. Carmen: Rise Stevens; Don José: Jan Peerce; Micaëla: Licia Albanese; Zuniga: Osie Hawkins; Moralès: Hugh Thompson. English translation of the libretto by Alice Berezowsky. RCA Victor Records, c. 1951.

22 Andean panpipes: three cortes (sizes). An example of the Peruvian "Toril" genre, in *conima* style. Performed by Patricia Hinostroza, Jesus Jaramillo (*chili* melody); Vanessa Luyo, Jose Carlos Pomari (*sanja* melody); Illich Ivan Montes, Hubert Yauri (*malta* melody). Followed by a traditional *sikuris* ensemble, including panpipes recorded in the Andean highlands, city of Puno, during the festival La Candelaria, in 1991. Courtesy of Raul Romero Cavallo, Centro de Etnomusicologia, Pontificia Universidad Catolica del Peru, Lima.

23 "Ma Ram" "Dancing Horse" (Thai *pî phât* ensemble). From *Traditional Music of Thailand*, 1968. Institute of Ethnomusicology, UCLA Stereo ier-7502. Courtesy of the UCLA Ethnomusicology Archives (David Morton Collection)

24 Paul Desmond "Take Five" (jazz). The Dave Brubeck Quartet (Dave Brubeck, Paul Desmond, Joe Morello, Gene Wright). Copyright © 1960, renewed 1988, Desmond Music Company (USA) Derry Music Company (world except USA); used with permission; all rights reserved.

25 "Maqam Rast" (naming intervals: mode and mood). Egyptian instrumental ensemble with vocal, c. 1958. Umm Kulthum, singer. "*Aruh li min*," composer: Riyad al-Sinbati; poet: `Abd al-Mun 'im al Saba 'i Sono Cairo.

26 "Hyōjō Netori" (Japanese *gagaku* ensemble). Gagaku Music Society of Tenri University, n.d. Courtesy of Koji Sato, Director, Gagaku Music Society of Tenri University.

27 "Te Kuki Airani nui Maruarua" (Polynesian homogenous choral song/chant from the Cook Islands, in the joyous old style called *ute*). Singers from the Cook Islands National Arts Theatre. From *Festival of Traditional Music: World of the South Pacific* (New York: Musical Heritage Society, c. 1974).

28 Witold Lutosławski, "Mini Overture" (1982). Meridian Arts Ensemble: Jon Nelson, Richard Kelley (trumpet), Daniel Grabois (horn), Benjamin Herrington (trombone), Raymond Stewart (tuba). Courtesy of Music Sales Corporation and Channel Classics CCS 2191, c. 1991.

29 "La Negra" From *Mariachi Music of Mexico* Cook 5014, c. 1954. Courtesy of Smithsonian Folkways Recordings. Used by permission.

30 Sargam (North Indian vocal solfège). From Bonnie C. Wade, *Khyāl: Creativity within North India's Classical Musical Tradition* (Cambridge:

Cambridge University Press, 1984). Cassette tape master in the collection of the author.

31 I Myoman Windha, "Jagra Parwat" from *Kreasi Baru for Gong Kebyar*. Vital Records 402.

32 "West End Blues" (New Orleans jazz). Louis Armstrong, trumpet, et al. Courtesy of MCA Universal.

33 "Marieke." Words and Music by Eric Blau, Jacques Brel, Gerard Jouannest. Recording and text translation courtesy of Suzanne Lake. Recorded by Suzanne Lake, *The Soul of Chanson*, CD. © Copyright 1968 Universal-MCA Music Publishing, a Division of Universal Studios, Inc. (ASCAP) International Copyright Secured. All rights reserved.

34 Frédéric Chopin, *Waltz in C-sharp Minor*. Performance by Jean Gray Hargrove. Recording courtesy of Jean Gray Hargrove.

35 Bruce Springsteen, "Born in the USA." Columbia CK 38653.

36 Dave Brubeck, "Three to Get Ready and Four to Go" (jazz). The Dave Brubeck Quartet (Dave Brubeck, Paul Desmond, Joe Morello, Gene Wright). Copyright © 1960, renewed 1988, Derry Music Company; used with permission; all rights reserved.

37 "Tar Road to Sligo" and "Paddy Clancy's Mug of Brown Ale" (Irish jigs). Becky Tracy, fiddle; Stan Scott, mandolin; Dora Hast, whistle. From *Jig Medley* cassette. Courtesy of Becky Tracy, Stan Scott, and Dora Hast.

38 "Makedonsko horo" (Bulgarian *tambura*). Recorded by Tsvetanka Varimezova, 29 December 2001. Courtesy of Tsvetanka Varimezo and Timothy Rice.

39 "Unnai Nambinen" (South Indian *Ādi tāla*). *Rāga Kirawāni* (21st *mela*). T. Vishwanathan, singer; David Nelson, *mṛdaṅgam*; Anantha Krishnan, *tāmbūra*. Music by T. M. Swami Pillay, Text by Muttutanuvar. Courtesy of Matthew Allen, T. Vishwanathan, David Nelson, Anantha Krishnan.

40 Richard Strauss, *Also Sprach Zarathustra*, excerpt. Columbia MK 35888, 1980.

41 "Seki no To" (Japanese *shamisen* and vocal). Example of *Tokiwazu*, a section from the *Kabuki* play *Tsumoru koi yuki no Seki no to*, music by Tobaya Richoo I, text by Takarada Jurai. 1784. From *1,000 Years of Japanese Classical Music*, vol. 7, *Tokiwazu, Tomimoto, Kiyomoto, Shinnai*. Nihon koten ongaku taikei. (Tokyo: Kodansha, 1980–82).

42 Balinese *jublag.* Recorded by Lisa Gold.

43 Western orchestra tuning process. University of California, Berkeley, Orchestra.

44 "Frère Jacques" ("*Are you sleeping?*"). Recorded by Viet Nguyen and Jane Chiu.

45 Western major scale. Recorded by Viet Nguyen and Jane Chiu.

46 "Oriental" scale. From *Cante Flamenco Agujetas en Paris* (Ocora, 1991).

47 Western vertical intervals.

48 Progression of pitches (roots of chords).

49 "Sumer is icumen in" (medieval European *rota*). Courtesy of the Chamber Chorus of the University of California, Berkeley, Paul Flight, director, 2001.

50 *Kotekan "norot"* (Balinese *gangsas*). Recorded by Lisa Gold.

51 *"Yaegoromo"* (Japanese *sankyoku* ensemble). Jiuta Yonin no Kai Ensemble (Tokyo: Ocora, n.d.).

52 Scottish bagpipe drone. Recording by John Pedersen. Courtesy of Lucia Comnes.

53 "Rāga Miyāṅ ki Ṭoḍi" (North Indian vocal). Dagar Brothers, CD 4137.

54 Ludwig van Beethoven, *Symphony No. 5*, excerpt. London Symphony Orchestra, Wyn Morris, conductor. MCA Classics, n.d.

55 Episode from *woi-meni-pele* (Kpelle epic performance). Liberian *Womi* epic pourer. Courtesy of Ruth Stone.

56 "The Great Ambush." Tsun-yuen Lui, Chinese *pipa*. Courtesy of Tsur-yuen Lui and the UCLA Archives of Ethnomusicology.

57 "Duke in the Land" (Trinidadian *calypso*). Julian Whiterose, 1914.

58 "Kumbaya." Kenyan. Courtesy of Greg Barz.

59 *"Riachao"* (Brazilian *capoeira*). São Bento Pequeno de Angola e São Bento Grande de Compasso. From *Capoeira: A Saga do Urucungo* (Luzes: Silvio Acaraje, n.d.).

Locations mentioned in this text are highlighted.

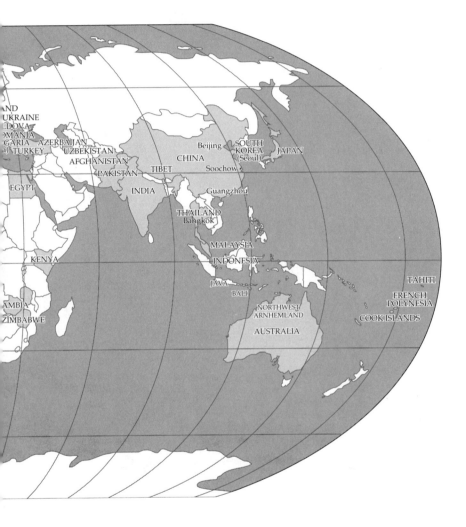

Thinking Musically

CHAPTER 1

Thinking about Music

∞

If you can speak you can sing; if you can walk you can dance.
(Zimbabwean Shona proverb)

All over the world, people make music meaningful and useful in their lives.
That statement encapsulates much of what ethnomusicologists are interested in and offers a framing perspective for many ways of thinking both about people and about music. In this chapter I shall explore each word in the statement with two purposes in mind: to suggest new ways you might think about music that you regularly hear, and to begin to expand your musical horizon. Because this is a teaching book, I shall also begin by speaking briefly about the transmission of music, the ways it is taught and learned.

PEOPLE

Music Makers. Who makes music in our familiar world? Music makers are individuals and groups, adults and children, female and male, amateurs and professionals. They are people who make music only for themselves, such as shower singers or secretly-sing-along-with-the-radio types, and they are performers, people who make music purposefully for others. They are people who make music because they are required to and people who do so simply from desire. Some music makers study seriously, while others are content to make music however they can, without special effort.

To think about music makers globally, you might ask whether music makers are regarded in any particular way in a particular place. At one end of a spectrum, some societies expect people who make music to be specialists, born into the role or endowed with a special capacity.

At the other end of that spectrum, in some societies it is assumed that the practice of music is a human capacity and that all people will express themselves musically as a normal part of life.

Local terminology is a clue to the ideas held about music makers. When you hear or use the word "musician," to what sort of music maker are you referring? When I ask this question of students in my courses, most reply with an impression clearly derived from the sphere of Western classical music. In this volume, however, I use the word **musician** more generically, to cover all people who experience music as a practice (figure 1.1).

Many questions about musicians embed them in their musical context. Who makes music with whom? Who learns music from whom? Who is permitted to be a teacher? Who can perform where? Who can perform for whom? Is anyone prohibited from making some particular type of music, and if so, why? Who plays which instrument, and why? Do musicians have high cultural status (i.e., is their music making highly valued by a group)? Do musicians have high social status (i.e., a high ranking in the society)?

ACTIVITY 1.1 *Make an inventory of music makers in your individual context. Do you ever make music? Do your friends? Some family members?*

Listeners.   When I speak about people making music meaningful and useful in their lives, I include people who "just" listen. They are, after all, most of the world's musically involved population. Listeners, like musicians, are consumers of music. They are the audience to which performers cater—patrons who are willing to pay to hear performances and buy recordings.

Answers to questions about listeners reveal a great deal about the musical context in which they live. Do they prefer to listen alone, or is listening a social activity? Is it more expensive to listen to one kind of music than another, and if so, what does that mean for the listener? Are certain types of listeners associated with certain types of music? Is a listening audience restricted by gender or religious belief or membership? Does a listening context foster immediate interaction between performer and listener?

ACTIVITY 1.2 *Agree or disagree with this statement: listening to music is different from hearing music. Think of that mood music in the elevator, the background music in shops, the radio playing to keep the painter company in the apartment next door.*

MUSIC

In Terms of Sound. I am standing at the edge of a body of water, the ripples sounding alternately like gentle lapping and heavy crashing waves. Nearby, hammers and electric saws are punctuating the air. Above me, soaring and dipping and singing a variety of songs are goldfinches and mockingbirds and cooing doves. The wind whistles across the land. Car horns toot in the distance. In this wonderful soundscape there is melody and rhythm. Can any of that be called *music?*

ACTIVITY 1.3 *To begin thinking musically, think about sound. Conduct some field research: taking pen and paper with you, listen for thirty minutes to the soundscape around you and keep a record. Any sound—a motorcycle roaring by, a cluster of people laughing, sounds of nature, the whirring of an elevator's approach, the selection on the radio of a passing motorist, the music you choose to play. Some of the sounds you hear must be what you would automatically call "music." Articulate how you distinguish between what is and what is not music.*

In fact, what is music? The ethnomusicologist John Blacking defined it as "humanly organized sound" (1977), but I suggest that we take that statement one step farther. "Music" is not only a thing—a category of organized sound, or compositions—but also a process. Every known group of people in the world exercises their creative imaginations to organize sound in *some way* that is different from the way they organize sound for speech.

Calling Something "Music." Having a word for a particular aesthetic category of organized sound that I as an individual think of as

FIGURE 1.1
Collage of music makers.

1.1a: Street musician: Youth playing didjeridu. (Photo by Lisa McCabe)

1.1b: Street musician: Man playing electrified lute. (Photo by Lisa McCabe)

1.1c: *Marika Kuzma, Director of Choruses, University of California, Berkeley.* (Photo by Peg Skorpinski)

1.1d: *Two members of a Chinese music troupe in Bangkok, Thailand. The writing on the drum stand says "Disciples of Lŭang Pù Sêng, Kalayaan Temple, Thonburi." The stand displays a photo of and offering to their teacher, who is a monk. They are performing at a blessing ceremony for the opening of a new music store, called Dr. Sax, owned by music professor Dr. Sugree Charoensoek. 1989.* (Courtesy of Deborah Wong)

1.1e: *Irish session: seisun in Ocean View, Miltown Malbay Co. Clare. Michael Falsey (pipes), Mary Anne Sexton (accordeon), Gabi Wolff (flute).* (© Peter Laban, Miltown Malbay Co. Clare)

"music" is by no means universal. None of the hundreds of First Nation groups have a word for "music," for instance. It is not set apart as a category; it is just there, and everyone participates in it. In India the word for music, *saṅgīta*, is used to encompass dance as well as music. In other places a word for "music" refers only to instrumental music. In the Islamic worldview, the mellifluous recitation of the sacred Koran (CD track 1), which many non-Muslim listeners have called "music," is not considered *musiqa*; *musiqa* is a category encompassing **genres** (that is, types of music) associated with secular life. Clearly, just because something sounds like music to me, I have no right to insist that it is "music" to someone else. It is the local or even personal idea that counts.

Christopher Small has taken the position that music is not a thing at all, but an activity, something that people do, and ethnomusicologists generally concur. He calls doing music "musicking": "to music is to take part, in any capacity, in a musical performance, whether by performing, by listening, by rehearsing or practicing, by providing material for performance (what is called composing), or by dancing" (1998: 9). He sometimes—and I always would—extends musicking to all the activities about which I wrote above under "People."

Musical Values. If I, in my American culture, use the expression "that's music to my ears," you will know that I have heard something I want to hear, or in terms of sound, something beautiful. Ideas about beauty are one aspect of a set of artistic values referred to as **aesthetics**—in this case, music aesthetics. Those ideas are not necessarily shared, even within one society. A letter to an editor about Trinidadian **steelband** encapsulates the obvious fact that a beautiful sound to one person is abominable to another (CD track 2, figure 1.2):

> Can beating is pan beating in any language and in any form. It does nobody any good, and when it is indulged in all day all night, day in and day out, it is abominable. . . . If it must continue and if by virtue of its alleged inherent beauty and charm it will someday bring popularity and fame to the island and a fortune to the beaters, then by all means let it go on—but in the forests and other desolate places. (C. W. Clarke, *Trinidad Guardian*, 6 June 1946)

While individual ethnomusicologists have personal ideas about musical beauty in terms of the quality of the sound (**timbre**) that is cultivated, it is a tenet of our field that we will keep our ears and minds open and respect the fact that many timbres are considered beautiful.

FIGURE 1.2 *Steeldrum. On left, Tom Miller, tenor pan. On right, Alan Light-ner, double seconds/pan.* *(Photo by Kathleen Karn)*

Aesthetic ideas are also expressed in terms of process, through the way music is composed and performed. In many folk music traditions in China each performer will "add flowers" by embellishing and vary-ing a melody, resulting in a personal style and voice. Amateur music groups, especially, expand on that process to shape a collective "sound" (CD track 3). The Venezuelan artist Cheo Navarro articulated the aes-thetic of *salsa* as "the rhythmic feel" resulting from the well-performed interlocking rhythmic patterns of the timbal, conga, and bongo drums (Berrios-Miranda 1999; figure 1.3, CD track 4). In North Indian instru-mental performance, a shifting relationship is desired between the two primary ensemble members—melodist and drummer—with the drum-mer shifting from supporting accompanist to soloist to competitor as a performance selection is improvised.

The aesthetically ideal process for performance of some types of Western classical music, on the other hand, is that a received (i.e., pre-composed) piece of music will be reproduced with a high level of tech-nical proficiency coupled with artistic expressivity; the composition will not be changed to any great extent. In contrast, the aesthetic process in-

FIGURE 1.3 Salsa *drummers. From left to right: on bongo, Shannon Dudley; on congas, Greg Campbell; on bongos, Marisol Berrios.* *(Courtesy of Marisol Berrios)*

volved in most popular music permits artists the freedom to render a piece in very distinctive ways.

Aesthetic ideas have a great deal to do with the nature of the musical content, and those same ideas might obtain in dance as well. In West African traditions, short segments (facets) are highly valued: Kpelle dance movements consist of short, quick, tightly orchestrated steps, for instance. In much African drumming, short rhythmic patterns are repeated in close coordination with other short rhythmic patterns, as an example from CD track 5 demonstrates. It is the process of interlocking the short segments that creates "the music"; the musical experience is a social experience. If, as in Christopher Small's terms, musicking articulates our ideal of human relationships, then this African aesthetic provides a wonderful example.

For many people, the highest value of music is placed on affect, that is, its expressive capacity. As one of my students put it, "It is music that makes me want to dance, or feel. It not only reminds me of times I have felt emotions, but it prompts me to feel emotions" (Lyndsey Brown, 2001). The first time I consciously thought about the tremendous power of music for affecting emotion was years ago when I watched the classic movie *Ben-Hur*. The chariot race between Ben-Hur and his adversary was nearing its climax. With whips cracking, horses' hooves pounding, chariot wheels clashing, crowds and the orchestra roaring, we in the theater could hardly stand the tension. Suddenly, the sound system failed. Without the furor of the music egging us and the action on, the race looked silly, for the emotional impact of the scene was expressed by the music. Contrasting utterly with that were the feelings that welled up in me as I heard "Taps" and the American national anthem as I stood with other countrymen in the military cemetery in Manila, the Philippines, where I was just after President Kennedy was assassinated in 1963. Yes, music has the power to move our hearts and minds.

ACTIVITY 1.4 *It is not always easy to express in words why you like or value a kind of music or a performance. Try it, with one piece of music you really love.*

∞

Student Lucia Comnes: "I feel that the youth in my community are drawn to this music [reggae] and culture because it is liberating. We are about to inherit this monster that is our society—including the government, the educational system, the work force, the media, the capitalist philosophy, the technology, the developed civilization, the destruction of the earth, the inequality, the separating illusions of racism, sexism, ageism, homophobia, etc. and the list goes on—I often find this overwhelming, confusing, and terrifying. When the communities at home and at school are not strong or secure, we yearn for another place that speaks to us deeply, a place that brings us to a higher consciousness. Reggae culture provides this for many—a place where people are brought together through music, music coming from the heart, speaking to the power of the people, music that is alive and encouraging, fulfilling and in the spirit of celebration" (2001).

Student Aron: "There is another subject to be very critically thought about, reflecting on the upper-middle-class white audience, joining or co-opting a poor black protest. This is not really talked about and there is so much to be addressed. As a white middle-class kid myself who listens to a lot of dance hall and reggae, I am constantly checking in with the fact that I can't call it mine. So reggae causes me to think. When you're in clubs and there are white and black audiences grooving to reggae, it is a lot more apparent and you are confronted with this" (2001).

∾

MEANING

That music is meaningful, no one doubts. However, great debates have ensued over whether the meaning resides in musical materials themselves or is ascribed to musical materials by someone for some particular reason. Is there something really martial about the music played by a brass band as an army marches by, or is that an association we have learned? Does a lullaby really put a child to sleep, or is it something else such as loving attention that lulls the child into secure rest? With most ethnomusicologists, I think the latter: people make music meaningful, whether that meaning is individual or communally agreed upon.

Music and Textual Meaning. Melody set to words constitutes much of the world's musical repertoire. Perhaps it is because everyone can sing, with or without an instrument. Perhaps it is because of the capacity of music to heighten the expressivity of a text. In the Baroque period (c. 1600–1750 C.E.) of European music, composers used what was called "word painting" to heighten expressivity in quite literal ways— a falling melody on the word *morire* (to die), for instance. Blues singers in America improvise expressively to elicit even more meaning from already meaningful texts.

Another reason for singing texts is the license it gives musicians to say something not permitted in ordinary speech. A great deal of covert and overt political protest has been delivered in song. In "Calypso Freedom," Sweet Honey in the Rock reminds listeners of the necessity of the civil rights movement of the 1960s while renewing the protest in 1989 with new text set to an old song (CD track 6).

ACTIVITY 1.5 *Find a song of political protest. Transcribe the lyrics and then listen to the musical setting. Do the musicians use the music in any purposeful way to deliver the message of the text?*

Through the ages narrators have told their tales musically. The Texas-Mexican *corrido* is a genre that has proven to be an effective avenue for protest, as well as a narrative. "The Ballad of César Chávez" (figure 1.4, CD track 7) relates an important event in American history: the march of that famed Mexican American leader in the struggle for rights for

El Corrido de César Chávez	*The Ballad of César Chávez*
En un día siete de marzo	*On the seventh day of March*
Jueves santo en la mañana,	*Good Thursday in the morning*
salió César de Delano	*César left Delano*
componiendo una campaña.	*Organizing a campaign.*
Compañeros campesinos	*Companion farmers*
este va a ser un ejemplo	*This is going to be an example*
esta marcha la llevamos	*This (protest) march we'll take*
hasta mero Sacramento.	*To Sacramento itself.*
Cuando llegamos a Fresno	*When we arrived in Fresno*
Toda la gente gritaba	*All the people chanted*
y que viva César Chávez	*Long live César Chávez*
y la gente que llevaba.	*And the people that accompany him.*

Nos despedimos de Fresno	We bid good-bye to Fresno
nos despedimos con fe	We bid good-bye with faith
para llegar muy contentos	So we would arrive contented
hasta el pueblo de Merced.	To the town of Merced.
Ya vamos llegando a Stockton	We are almost in Stockton
ya mero la luz se fue	Sunlight is almost gone
pero mi gente gritaba	But the people shouted
sigan con bastante fe.	Keep on with lots of faith.
Cuando llegamos a Stockton	When we arrived at Stockton
los mariachis nos cantaban	The mariachis were singing
que viva César Chávez	Long live César Chávez
y la Virgen que llevaba.	And the Virgin of Guadalupe.

(The selection on CD track 7 ends here; following is the remainder of the corrido.)

Contratistas y esquiroles	Contractors and scabs
ésta va a ser una historia	This is going to be your story
ustedes van al infierno	You will all go to hell
y nosotros a la gloria.	And we will go to heaven.
Ese Señor César Chávez	That Mr. César Chávez
él es un hombre cabal	Is a very strong man
quería verse cara a cara	He wanted to speak face to face
con el gobernador Brown.	With Governor Brown.
Oiga, Señor César Chávez,	Listen, Mr. César Chávez,
su nombre que se pronuncia	Your name is well known
en su pecho usted merece	On your chest you well deserve
la Virgen de Guadalupe.	The Virgin of Guadalupe.

FIGURE 1.4 *Song text: "The Ballad of César Chávez." Texas-Mexican corrido. (From Las Voces de los Campesinos: Francisco García and Pablo and Juanita Saludado Sing Corridos about the Farm Workers and Their Union. Reproduced with permission from the Center for the Study of Comparative Folklore and Mythology, UCLA, FMSC-1.)*

migrant farmworkers. In spring 1965 the first major strike against grape growers took the form of a march from Delano, California, to the state's capital, Sacramento, to meet with then-Governor Edmund "Pat" Brown. Because of the religious orientation of Mexican culture, the march became a nexus of the religious tradition of pilgrimage and the contemporary form of demonstration. References to the Lady of Guadalupe allude to a major shrine in Mexico, the Basilica of the Lady of Guadalupe.

Among the narrative genres that link music to text for the expression and heightening of meaning, musical drama is perhaps the single best example. In Balinese theater the nexus between music and the narrative both in terms of mood and action is so close and so familiar to audiences that the dramatic meaning is automatically remembered when the same musical material occurs without words in a nontheatrical context.

We might assume that a sung text is meant to be understood. Not necessarily so! Even when a Central Javanese **gamelan** (ensemble) includes vocalists, the text they sing may not be immediately intelligible. Not only do their voices blend into the greater ensemble sound, but the poems are usually in old Javanese language that few listeners know (CD track 8; figure 1.5). For the few who can understand, the meaning lies both in the text itself and in the singing of it; for the less knowledgeable, the meaning lies in the recognition that an old text is being sung, in the assurance that tradition continues.

FIGURE 1.5 *Central Javanese* gamelan *playing for* wayang kulit *(leather puppet play).* (Photo by Kathleen Karn)

Sometimes melody is sung to text that is not linguistically meaningful—syllables such as "fa la la" in English carols. You might hear people use the phrase "meaningless syllables" for such text, but ethnomusicologists no longer do so. Syllables assumed to be meaningless have been found upon further investigation to be archaic language, or mystically meaningful. Instead, ethnomusicologists refer to the syllables as **vocables**, suggesting their function in the music. The text of CD track 9, a Navajo corn-grinding song recorded in 1940 with the lead singer Joe Lee, in Lukachukai, Arizona, consists completely of vocable phrases.

Aghei ha yana ghei aghei	*Aghei ha yana ghei aghei*
Aghei yolei yolei hanei-hana	*Aghei yolei yolei hanei-hana*
O—weya hena a nana	*O—weya hena a nana ghei aghei*
Aghei ha yana ghei aghei	*Aghei ha yana ghei aghei.*

The opposite of texted song without linguistic meaning is **program music**—instrumental music without a text that is treated as if it had one. With its many narrative genres and operatic styles, Chinese music, even instrumental music, is very text-oriented. A title such as "Plum Blossoms" is subject to interpretation, but each instrumentalist may express it differently. The "text" is not in the musical sound but in the musicians' and listeners' meaningful interpretations of the title.

Music as Text. In a subtle pairing of melody and text, the singer of the Alha epic in North India might deliver the bravado words of a warrior to the familiar melody of a woman's song genre. The bravado words are a text certainly, but so is the musical commentary on his womanly personality. Such subtlety requires a knowledgeable audience to be understood.

As that example illustrates, music can acquire meaning from the situation in which it is made or heard, and then become a kind of text in itself. Its meaning is then "situated." Once you have learned to associate the melody of "We Shall Overcome" with protest, for instance, you do not have to hear any text to understand its situated meaning. A person in Korea who says, "I'm going to an orchestra concert tonight," has immediately asserted an association with a type of music that has high cultural status in Korea as well as in Western cultures; even the mention of orchestral music is a kind of subtext.

Another example of situated meaning: my favorite theory about the reason that we continue to hate or love (if not get stuck in) the popular music of our teenage years is that we absorbed that music when we were experiencing love and other emotions intensely as adolescents. It is not only the style of the music that stays with us but also the memory of the meaning it had at that crucial time in our lives.

∾

Student Lisa McCabe: "Music helps me understand myself. I know if I instinctively want to hear a certain sad song, that something must be bothering me. Or if I want to hear a song that reminds me of home, I miss my friends."

Student Shanesha Brooks: "I find that if a song that I wouldn't normally listen to is playing on the radio during a time when I am having a good time, it is attached to that time and therefore it has more meaning than it would otherwise have."

∾

USE

Music is also meaningful because it functions in some way in people's lives. Music defines, represents, symbolizes, expresses, constructs, mobilizes, incites, controls, transforms, unites, and so much more. People make music useful in those ways.

I have asked many people about the place of music in their lives. Many have replied: "Oh, I'm not interested in music at all." Then they admit regularly listening to music in their cars, occasionally going to a performance, dancing on a date, exercising with a Walkman, or otherwise putting music into their lives. This they may categorize as enjoyment, as entertainment rather than musical activity. However they regard it, they are making music useful.

Music can be made to function in multiple ways. As a mode of interaction among people, it serves a social function. Arousing public sentiment is a political function. Praising God is a spiritual function. Creating a romantic mood is an affective function. Untold numbers of people make a living from music—from paid performers to students who work in music libraries and record shops. Students in one of my courses had these comments to add: "Involvement in music looks good on a college application; that's a status function, a statement of self-worth." "Music helps me understand other people and their actions, to place myself in another person's shoes." "It's a stress reliever." "It quiets my anger and otherwise improves my mood." "Music helps me fo-

cus while doing repetitive tasks." "I remember things through song."
"I use music to escape from chaos!"

One of the most significant uses to which people put music is to express an identity. Performers do this to establish an individual identity
as a musician, of course, but music can also be emblematic of a group—
a college, as in a school song; a sporting team, as in "We Are Family"
(as "claimed" by the 1979 Pittsburgh Pirates baseball team); a heritage
group, as in the Polish polka or the blues; a nationality, as in a national
anthem. The meaning of such music is highly situated and useful for
purposes ranging from contestation to solidarity.

ACTIVITY 1.6 *Think about the music in your life. Does it
have some meaning for you, beyond its musical qualities? How
do you use music? Can you distinguish between its meaning and
its function?*

In the real world and now in the virtual world, however, music can
be heard in vastly different places and at any time. It can easily be experienced as utterly decontextualized—divorced from its time and
place, cut off from its original makers, meanings, and uses as musicians
collect sounds from all over the world to create, as the singer Marc Anthony put it, "world music in a Long Island basement" (Buia 2001: 10).
We can no longer assume that ethnic musical materials will serve as
markers of particular ethnic identities, for example. Such globally
shared music (or "global music," as most ethnomusicologists call it) is
constantly recontextualized by those who listen to it, given new meanings, and made to perform new—as well as the same old—functions.
Other musical boundaries are being superseded as well. Musical ownership is challenged by sampling. Boundaries between musical genres
such as jazz, rock, and classical are routinely breached. The creative process continues as music and music making become what people want
them to be.

TRANSMISSION

One of the most crucial factors for music anywhere is the process by
which it is taught and learned. The means by which this happens are
oral and visual (usually referred to as written). In ethnomusicology we

have become increasingly careful to distinguish between oral and aural transmission. **Oral transmission** takes the perspective of the teacher and implies interaction between teacher and learner. **Aural transmission** takes the perspective of the learner, who hears the music through some aural source. Written transmission depends on notation of some sort; a number of systems exist that have been developed according to need. In this section I shall briefly address these processes of transmission.

Oral and Aural Transmission. Most music is learned aurally—both by intentional listening and by osmosis, that is, by absorbing what we hear around us. This was already the case before the early twentieth century, when radio and recordings expanded the potential material that was available for learning. The mass media are without doubt the single greatest teaching force, playing an enormously significant role in the transmission of musical knowledge.

Where music is taught primarily by oral transmission, the teacher plays a significant role, as a repository of knowledge and technique, the individual responsible for musical quality, and often a guide in life (as the Indian *guru* is). The availability of recordings can change the degree of dependence of a pupil on a teacher, as well as the degree of control a teacher has over musical knowledge, but personal instruction provides a qualitatively different learning experience. Student-teacher relationships vary greatly. Particularly where music is being transmitted orally, but within a written tradition as well, a teacher might or might not be willing to make verbal explanations, preferring instead that the student listen, watch, and do.

A student of mine, Nontapat Nimityongskul, told me in 1999, "There are two main ways we can keep music. One is to write it down. The other is to know it in your heart." Nontapat raises an issue concerning oral and aural versus written transmission. Will music learned aurally be remembered and preserved? Quite possibly it will fade from memory, unless one or all of three conditions exist. The first and most necessary condition is that one intends to remember the music precisely as learned. This is a matter of personal or group motivation. The motivation would exist, for example, when there is a fear that incorrect rendering will cause some disaster.

The second condition is a system for learning the music so thoroughly that it is not likely to be forgotten. The most evidently successful such system was devised for the chanting of religious texts that have survived in Hindu Indian culture since the Vedic period (roughly 1500–500 B.C.E.). Without any reference to written materials, the chants have been transmitted from Brahmin priests to young Brahmin boys through untold numbers of generations. The teaching priest has his pupils repeat the sentences of the sacred text, using a well worked out memorization technique: using patterns that arrange the words of sentences in different order, the text is repeated endlessly until truly absorbed. Among the several patterns, the *krama* pattern is a simple one: *ab, bc, cd, de,* and so on. Each letter (*a, b, c,* etc.) indicates a word (CD track 10). Thus the sentence "Why am I doing this?" would be chanted as follows: "Why am / am I / I doing / doing this?" With innumerable repetitions, you will remember the sentence well.

ACTIVITY 1.7 *CD track 10 begins with* mālá. *Listen to CD track 10, the teaching of Vedic recitation, until you can follow these patterns. The line of text is: "Devīṃ vacam ajanayanta devās tām vísvarūpāh paśavo vadanti / sā no mandreṣam ūrjaṃ duhānā dhenur vāg asmān upa suṣṭutaitu" ("The gods gave birth to the goddess of speech, spoken by animals in all forms; this cow, lowing pleasantly, who gives strengthening libation with her milk, as speech when well spoken should come to us"). First the priest reads the line as a normal sentence. Then he announces each pattern and recites the line in that pattern. (Endings of some words change, by the Sanskrit rules of connection.)*

krama *pattern:*   ab / bc / cd / de / . . .

mālā *pattern:*   ab / ba / ab / bc / cb / bc / cd / dc / . . .

jaṭā *pattern:*   abbaab / bccbbc / cddccd / deedde / . . .

Once you understand this technique, make up your own short sentence and subject it to the patterns. Memorized in this manner, it is no doubt a sentence you will remember for a long time.

The third condition is a system of reinforcement: a system that assures that memory of the music will be periodically renewed. "Oldies" radio broadcasts perform this function; recurring music in a religious calendrical cycle does as well, such as carols sung at Christmas or prayers chanted at Passover. In some situations, the responsibility for reinforcing memories is taken by institutions. In Java (Indonesia), musicians at the royal courts hold rehearsals expressly to maintain musical compositions and choreographies that are transmitted mainly through oral tradition. Referring to something written is another way to renew the memory periodically.

The best way to maintain musical memory is to have a sound recording available, for so much is excluded from even the most comprehensive system of notation—sensual vocal production that is characteristic of a style, for instance. Preservation was an unintended achievement of the recording industry when it began to record all kinds of musics in the early twentieth century as a way to sell the new phonograph machines. Using that technology, ethnomusicologists, folklorists, and some anthropologists have been motivated to preserve the world's musical treasures, and there are now numerous sound archives around the globe. Touching stories circulate about groups whose traditional music no longer exists for some reason—radical change from international influence or memory loss where no system of reinforcement was in place—but recovery and revival is possible through recordings that someone deposited in an archive.

Written Transmission.   The nature of a notation system depends on the purpose people intend it to serve, and numerous types are in use around the world. If any musician wants to write a brief reminder of music already held in memory, a minimalist notation will suffice, recording only the musician's choice of crucial information. A musician who wants to prescribe in writing what someone else is to play or sing needs a detailed, prescriptive type of notation. That is the intention of Western staff notation.

Between minimalist and prescriptive notation lies the notation for the Chinese zither-type instrument the *qin* (pronounced "chin," figure 1.6). Like other **tablature**-type notations, it is intended to transmit per-

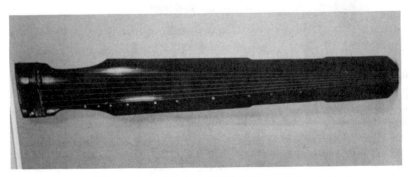

FIGURE 1.6   *Chinese qin.*   *(Courtesy of UCLA Ethnomusicology Archives)*

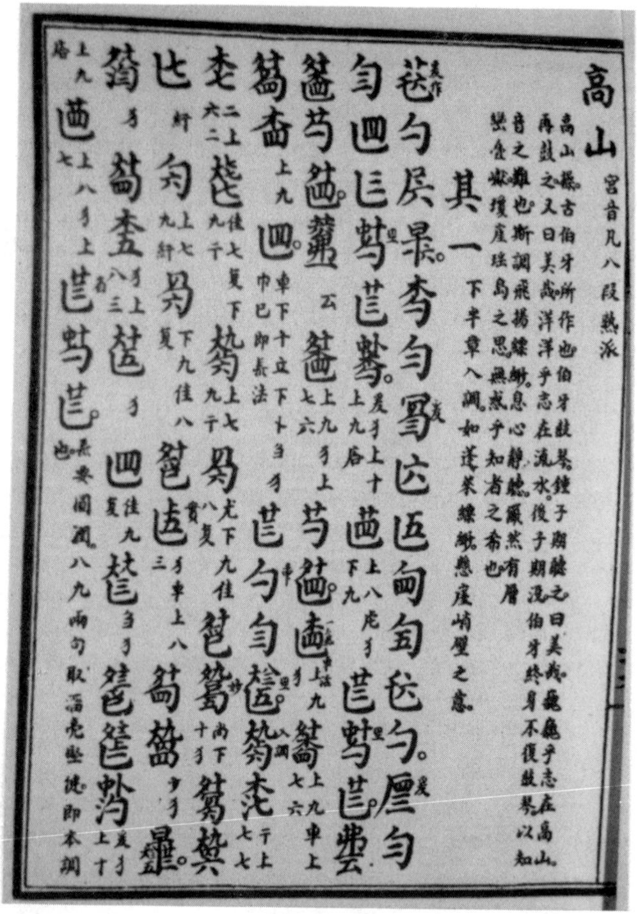

FIGURE 1.7 Qin *notation of "High Mountain."* *(Courtesy of UCLA Ethnomusicology Archives)*

forming instructions. Reproduced in figure 1.7 is the beginning of a piece, "High Mountain." The title of the piece is written on the far right column, and some information about it is given in the ensuing columns toward the left. Written Chinese language starts at the right, top to bottom; the notation of the piece follows that pattern, beginning in the seventh column, toward the middle of the page. Basically, the notation specifies left- and right-hand playing techniques and the strings on which they are to be executed. Figure 1.8 shows the right-hand tech-

	At the beginning of the piece (Column 1) only right hand techniques are required.
乇	Thumb pushes the string and comes to rest against the next string without sounding it.
勹	Middle finger pulls the string.
尸	Thumb pulls string with nail.
早	"Chord" from 2 simultaneous techniques.
ㄴ	Index finger pushes string with tip of fingernail.
写	Middle finger pushes string with tip of fingernail.
厂	Index finger executes two ㄴ in succession.

FIGURE 1.8 *Right hand qin techniques.* *(Chart by Jane Chiu, Viet Nguyen, and Pamela Han)*

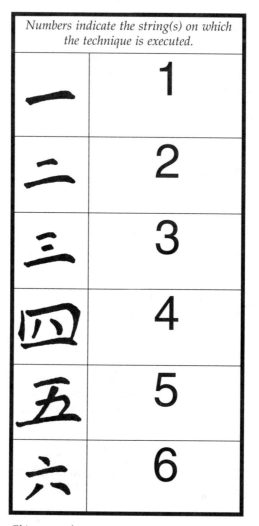

Numbers indicate the string(s) on which the technique is executed.	
一	1
二	2
三	3
四	4
五	5
六	6

FIGURE 1.9   *Chinese numbers.*   *(Chart by Jane Chiu, Viet Nguyen, and Pamela Han)*

niques required in the first column of notation of the piece. Figure 1.9 shows the Chinese numbers used to indicate the six strings of the instrument. Figure 1.10 shows how the techniques and numbers are combined in the notation.

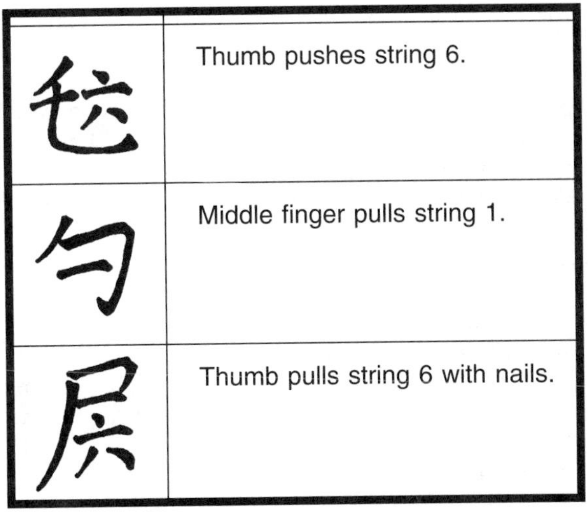

扺	Thumb pushes string 6.
勹	Middle finger pulls string 1.
戻	Thumb pulls string 6 with nails.

FIGURE 1.10 *Techniques and string numbers combined in* qin. *(Chart by Jane Chiu, Viet Nguyen, and Pamela Han)*

ACTIVITY 1.8 *Try copying at least half the notation in figure 1.7, to experience the flow of it. Then, using the guides in figures 1.8 and 1.9, try following the instructions it gives, playing some stringed instrument.*

What does this notation not tell you? That is, what is left for the teacher to transmit, or the player to interpret? This notation is descriptive, rather than prescriptive.

Notation is a kind of access to information. Whereas in an orally transmitted musical tradition the teacher controls whether or not a pupil may learn something, writing the music down makes it more accessible to greater numbers of people. Unlike in Western music, where all voices and instruments use staff notation (though a few instruments, notably guitar, also use a specialized tablature), in Japan each traditional instrument has its own system of notation. Standardized notation assumes that the music is to be shared among the general music-

1. The basic unit is a staff of five lines (▤); staves meant to be read simultaneously are joined by a vertical line at the left margin.
2. Individual musical sounds are represented by notes. ♩ ♩
3. Pitch is indicated by placing notes both on staff lines and in spaces between staff lines. ▤
4. Melodic contour is visible: Even if pitches cannot be identified, the rising and falling of the pitches can be followed.
5. When multiple musical parts are intended to be sounded together, they are aligned vertically.
6. Rhythm is shown by altering the appearance of notes. "Black" notes (with filled-in noteheads) are of shorter duration than "white" notes. A flag on the stem (♪) attached to a note shortens the duration. Additional time on the pitch is indicated by a dot after the note. For example:

    ♩ = 1 count
    ♪ = ½ count (half-counts are often linked by a beam ♫)
    ♩. = 1.5 counts
    ♩ = 2 counts
    ♩. = 3 counts

7. Meter (grouping of counts) is shown by vertical lines called bar lines. The space between two bar lines is called a measure. (In "Aloha Oe" each measure consists of four counts.) See chapter 3.

FIGURE 1.11 *Basic Guideline to Western Staff Notation*

reading public, whereas the Japanese system is tailored to in-group exclusivity.

The five-line **staff notation** system is so detailed that it requires a literacy that is specifically musical. With colonialism, however, its use was disseminated so widely in the world that it now constitutes a kind of international musical language. Because learning some of its basic principles can be of great help as a tool for musical communication, I give a brief guide here. An explanatory list of a few basic elements is given in figure 1.11, and others are added in figure 1.12, a sample of Western notation featuring a portion of the song "Aloha Oe," composed by Queen Liliuokalani of Hawaii (1838–1917).

An adage often voiced by one of my former teachers, Mantle Hood, is one I endorse: "A written tradition is only as strong as the oral tradition that supports it." If you have tried to read any notation system

FIGURE 1.12 *Western notation through "Aloha Oe."* *(with the assistance of Joseph Dales)*

without some further verbal explanation and hearing what is notated, you can recognize that to be true. In the end, an interplay between the oral/aural and written transmission of music is the reality for many musicians.

In this chapter I have introduced briefly the interests of ethnomusi-cologists in exploring how people all over the globe make music mean-ingful and useful in their lives. Instruments through which people make music are the subject of chapter 2.

Thinking about Instruments

∞

The countless and varied musical instruments that have existed through time are evidence of how people make music meaningful and useful in their lives. Because people have taken them wherever they have gone— for signals in war, for entertainment on expeditions, as items for trade, as gifts for foreign potentates—instruments also provide evidence of cultural diffusion. A notice posted by Craig McCrae on the Society for Ethnomusicology internet list offers an excellent example of this, with the accordion as example:

> One vital but little-known accordion tradition is found in the Khorezm region of Uzbekistan, in recent centuries seat of the Khiva khanate and an important center of high civilization since ancient times. The most typical Khorezmian ensembles combine the diatonic accordion with vocals, *doyra* (frame drum) and the Azerbaijani *tar* (a plucked, fretted lute with sympathetic strings, a bit smaller than the Iranian *tar*). . . . Russian colonists brought the accordion to the region in the late nineteenth century and the locals quickly adopted it for their own use. A high point in Khorezmian accordion history was in the 1930s when Soviets organized women's ensembles with forty or fifty accordions. (27 July 2000; cited with permission)

When people design and craft instruments, they both express cultural values and create musical practices through them. One basic question is whether instruments should be standardized. "Definitely!" say music makers and instrument makers wherever mass production and ensemble practice foster standardization. "Definitely not!" says the sitārist in India. "Add a string for me" (CD track 11). Most Indian music ensembles are small, and mass production of instruments is still low, so the idea of idiosyncratic instruments flourishes.

"Standardize the pitch of all instruments in this ensemble for me," says a Javanese purchaser to a smithy, "but make its tuning slightly different from the tuning of all other *gamelans*" (CD track 8). Where ensemble-specific pitch is an ideal, individuals in Java do not bring their own personal instrument to play in a *gamelan*; instead, they gather to play a set owned by a person, company, or club.

Indeed, instruments are items of expressive culture as well as material culture, works of art, symbols, technological inventions, tools for earning a livelihood. In this chapter I examine various ways in which people have thought about instruments, considering them first as physical objects apart from the music made with them, then as instruments in music, that is, as people use them musically. I include both voices and bodies among musical instruments.

INSTRUMENTS AS OBJECTS

Ideas about Types of Instruments. In two of the world's oldest civilizations—China and India—musical instruments have for millenia been considered particularly significant items of culture. While individual instruments had their specific meanings and uses, in China and India people also thought sytematically about them to develop **classification** systems for instrument types.

The ancient Chinese classification system resonated with the value that culture placed on nature. Chinese classified their instruments according to the natural material that produced each instrument's sound. The "eight sounds" (*ba yin*) were those of metal, stone, skin, vegetable gourd, bamboo, wood, silk, and earth (i.e., pottery). As shown in figure 2.1, the sounds were associated with cardinal directions and seasons. When musicians performed on specified instruments, the "eight sounds" were incorporated into significant rituals—not to provide musical variety, but to manifest a link with nature (CD track 12).

ACTIVITY 2.1 *Identify the natural sounds in CD track 12, Confucian ritual music. It originated in China but has been preserved in Korea, as* a–ak.

The *ba yin* classification system has fallen out of use, but the phrase "silk and bamboo" (*sizhu*) is still widely used in Chinese music to designate a string and wind ensemble. The phrase still names natural ma-

Ba yin system of instrument classification from
the Zhou Dynasty (c. 1000–200 BCE)

Type	Direction	Season	Instruments
Metal	West	Autumn	Bell-chimes
Stone	Northwest	Autumn to Winter	Stone-chimes
Skin	North	Winter	Drums
Gourd	Northeast	Winter to Spring	Mouth organ
Bamboo	East	Spring	Flutes, pipes
Wood	Southeast	Spring to Summer	Wooden tiger (scraper)
Silk	South	Summer	Zithers
Earth	Southwest	Summer to Autumn	Ocarinas, vessel flutes

FIGURE 2.1.   *The ancient Chinese* ba yin *instrument classification system.*

terials, but the intention now is to suggest a pleasing combination of different timbres (CD track 3).

Scholars in ancient India also cultivated an intellectual tradition of systematic thinking. They loved to classify and devised a variety of exhaustive categorizations—from character types in drama (in the *Nātya Sāstra* treatise) to physical positions in lovemaking (in the *Kāma Sūtra*). The classification system for musical instruments, dating from the fourth century B.C.E. and still viable today, identifies four basic types, according to the primary sound-producing medium: the vibrating body of the instrument itself, a vibrating membrane, a vibrating string, and a vibrating column of air.

In the European system of classification, there are four groups of instruments, based on the selection in the largest ensemble, an orchestra: strings, winds, percussion, and keyboard (figures 2.2 to 2.6). Wind instruments are also referred to in more specific categories, brass and woodwind. This system mixes the criteria for classification: strings and winds name the sound-producing medium; percussion and keyboard refer to the means of playing; and brass and woodwind pertain to the material of construction.

Nineteenth-century Europeans, in the interest of science (but to a large extent as a result of imperialistic colonialism), began to gather instruments from around the world and to deposit them in museum col-

FIGURE 2.2   *European instrument classification system: Strings. From left to right: Sophia Hanae Kessinger, Hoon Ku Lee (violin), Judy Minn (cello), Devin Kha Lac Tim (viola).*   *(Photo by Kathleen Karn)*

FIGURE 2.3   *European instrument classification system: Winds (Brass). From left to right: Michael Fraser (tuba), Christy Dana (trumpet), Karen Baccaro (trumpet), Beth Milne (horn), Suzanne Mudge (trombone).*   *(Photo by Kathleen Karn)*

FIGURE 2.4   *European instrument classification system: Winds (Woodwinds). From left to right: Flutes and oboes played by members of the UC Berkeley University Symphony Orchestra.   (Photo by Kathleen Karn)*

FIGURE 2.5   *European instrument classification system: Persussion. From left to right: Chimes, snare drum, cymbal, field drum, xylophone.   (Photo by Kathleen Karn)*

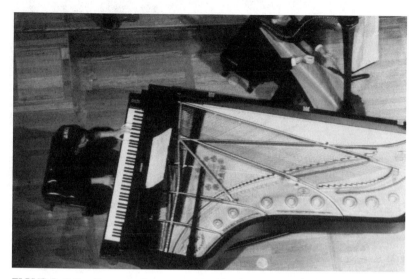

FIGURE 2.6   *European instrument classification system: Keyboard (and string). Nalini Gwynne (piano), Henry Spiller (harp).*   *(Photo by Kathleen Karn)*

lections, where they were documented as physical objects rather than meaningful items of culture. The task of cataloguing them presented a challenge. While efficient in their own musical context, the basic European criteria were too inconsistent to be useful for scientific classification. In the late nineteenth century, searching for a consistent system, the Belgian curator Victor Mahillon turned to the ancient Indian system with its one consistent criterion: the primary sound-producing medium of the instrument. As adapted, the categorical terms are as follows. An instrument whose body vibrates to produce sound is an **idiophone** (from the Latin *idem*, the thing itself). An instrument on which a vibrating membrane produces sound is a **membranophone**. A vibrating string produces the sound on a **chordophone**, while vibrating air is the primary sound-producing medium on an **aerophone** (see figure 2.7). Some instruments draw on more than one sound source, but this system designates only the primary one.

Early in the twentieth century, the German scholars Curt Sachs and Erich von Hornbostel espoused and expanded Mahillon's system, which is now used by museums and scholars worldwide. For greater specificity, they devised criteria for distinguishing instruments within each of the four major categories. A complete explanation of the system is found in Baines and Wachsmann (1961); here I provide only a few helpful definitions from that source. Note particularly the numbering system in the list below and the consistency from category to category, to the extent possible. For examples of instruments in the categories, see Figure 2.7.

1. Idiophones are subdivided by playing technique.
   11 Struck
   12 Plucked
   13 Friction
   14 Blown

2. Membranophones are subdivided first by playing technique.
   21 Struck
   22 Plucked
   23 Friction
   24 Singing membranes

Beyond further subdivision by shape, as shown in Figure 2.7, membranophones are then subdivided by number of heads and playing method.

3. Chordophones are subdivided by construction.
   31 A **zither** (simple chordophone) consists solely of a string bearer; the strings are parallel to the sounding body and run almost the entire length of the instrument.
   32 Composite chordophones
      321 A **lute** has a neck along which strings run, and the plane of the strings runs parallel with the sound table
      321.1 **Lyres,** classified as a type of lute, are important in Africa. The strings are attached to a yoke, which lies in the same plane as the sound table and consists of two arms and a crossbar.
      322 On a **harp** the plane of the strings lies at right angles to the sound table, and a line joining the lower ends of the strings points toward the neck.

All chordophones are further subdivided by playing technique. In ordinary conversation we are likely to refer to those techniques as struck, plucked, and bowed.

4. Aerophones are subdivided into
   41 Free aerophones and
   42 Wind instruments proper, on which the column of air is confined

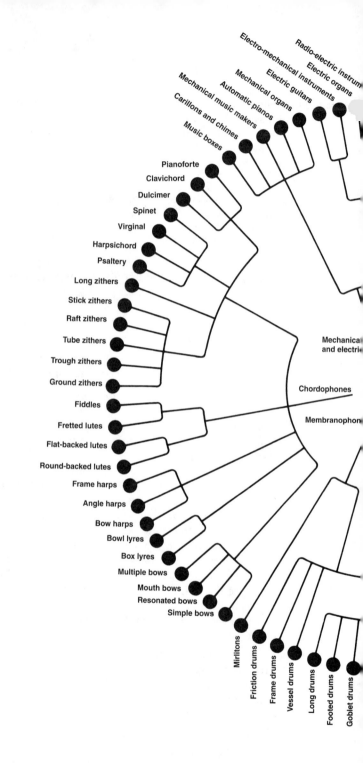

Radio-electric instrum
Electric organs
Electro-mechanical instruments
Electric guitars
Mechanical organs
Electric organs
Automatic pianos
Mechanical music makers
Carillons and chimes
Music boxes

Pianoforte
Clavichord
Dulcimer
Spinet
Virginal
Harpsichord
Psaltery
Long zithers
Stick zithers
Raft zithers
Tube zithers
Trough zithers
Ground zithers
Fiddles
Fretted lutes
Flat-backed lutes
Round-backed lutes
Frame harps
Angle harps
Bow harps
Bowl lyres
Box lyres
Multiple bows
Mouth bows
Resonated bows
Simple bows

Mechanical
and electri

Chordophones

Membranophon

Miritons
Friction drums
Frame drums
Vessel drums
Long drums
Footed drums
Goblet drums

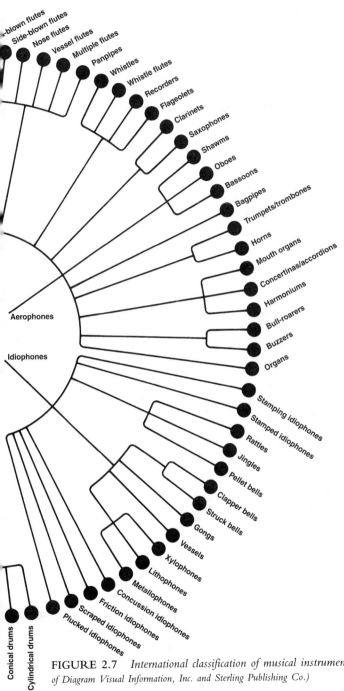

FIGURE 2.7 *International classification of musical instruments.* (*By permission of Diagram Visual Information, Inc. and Sterling Publishing Co.*)

421 On **flutes** a stream of air is directed against an edge.

422 On **reed pipes** the air stream has, through means of a reed placed at the head of the instrument, intermittent access to the column of air that is to be made to vibrate. Reed pipes are subdivided into:

422.1 **Double reeds**, on which a double layer of reed vibrates against itself

422.2 **Single reeds**, which vibrate against a plane

422.2 **Free reeds**, where a reed secured inside vibrates freely.

423 **Horn** and **trumpet**-type instruments, on which the air stream passes through the player's vibrating lips, so gaining intermittant access to the air column that is to be made to vibrate

Updating the Sachs-Hornbostel system calls for some adjustments, because it is designed only for acoustically generated sounds. Figure 2.7 includes **mechanical** and **electrical instruments.** A category of **corpophones** is another possibility, to include handclapping, finger snapping, body slapping, and the like into the system. In addition, the idea of membrane as animal skin requires stretching to include fiberglass heads of drums in the category of membranophones. While a number of instruments are hybrids and do not fit neatly into the categories of the Sachs-Hornbostel system, it continues to be extremely useful for the study of musical instruments.

ACTIVITY 2.2 *To correlate the numerical listing of the Sachs-Hornbostel system with Figure 2.7, add the numerals (1.1, 1.2, etc.) to the figure.*

Then experiment with devising a classification system for electronophones. Start by listing a few instruments you think belong in this category and work from there.

A number of relatively more contemporary ideas about grouping musical instruments are in use, meant not for worldwide comparative study but for local purposes. The Kpelle of West Africa, for example, categorize instruments by playing technique, as either struck (including plucked strings and drums) or blown. In Javanese *gamelan* the two major groupings are "loud-playing" (drums and louder bronze instruments) and "soft-playing" (flute, strings, and quieter bronze instruments). Those Javanese groupings are explained by historians as dating to the use of different ensembles for different performance contexts, but instruments from the two groupings have probably been combined in ensembles for about four hundred years.

The West African Igbo provide two conjunct systems for categorizing their musical instruments: according to the sounding material or the technique of sound production (Nzewi 1991: 57). At the same time they recognize sociocultural musical importance informed by variety and popularity, as follows.

1. The most popular and varied are the wooden, metal, and membrane instruments. Without producing definite pitches, these are capable of a wide range of phonic manipulation: to "sing," to "talk," and to play percussion roles in ensembles. Nzewi uses the term *melorhythm instruments* for these.

2. The second in importance are blown instruments, which are melody or phonic-effects-producing instruments.

3. Next are the shaken and pot instruments, which play percussive roles in ensembles.

4. Finally there are plucked (soft-toned) melody instruments, which are played primarily as solo instruments.

ACTIVITY 2.3 *Choose an instrument in each of the four basic categories of the Sachs-Hornbostel classification system that you see pictured in this book. Classify each of them in the other systems discussed above.*

Classification systems facilitate the comparison of instruments of the same basic type as they are found in various places around the world. One need only think of lute-type instruments, which most historians agree originated in the Middle East and spread gradually by the process of diffusion. Middle Eastern plucked lutes traveled different routes across the continent of Asia—east to China, west to Europe and beyond, becoming the Chinese *pipa*, the guitar, and the mariachi *vihuela* and *gui-*

tarrón, respectively, all of which you will see pictured and hear on selections later in this volume. A Middle Eastern bowed lute is the origin of the fiddle/violin, which, recycled back to Asia, was adopted into contemporary Middle Eastern and Indian music.

Ideas about Particular Instruments. Some instruments carry extramusical associations so clear and strong that the mere sound of them will transmit meaning to anyone in a knowledgeable group. The *didjeridu* (CD track 13, figure 1.1b), used as background music in television promotionals, evokes images of the Australian outback, *Crocodile Dundee*, or the lone Aboriginal on walkabout. Because of its historical association with court culture, European classical music imparts high class status in advertisements for expensive automobiles and expensive perfumes. The saxophone connotes "cool": a student, Tamina Spurney, noted, "When I hear it, I think of jazz and sunglasses and nightclubs and sophistication" (2001).

> **ACTIVITY 2.4** *Identify examples of extramusical associations with instruments. Listen and watch for these associations in TV ads and other contexts.*

Spiritual Associations. We find throughout the world the idea of an instrument's giving voice to a sacred spirit. In the Poro or Sande secret society of the Kpelle people of West Africa, an official plays pottery flutes to produce the voice of the spirits. In Buddhism, the conch shell produces the voice of Buddha symbolically; the call on CD track 14 invites monks to assemble at a Tibetan monastery temple at dawn. Not the voice of a sacred spirit, but a spiritual connection with nature and Zen Buddhist meditation, distinguishes the Japanese *shakuhachi* (figure 2.8; CD track 15).

Religious associations suggest many other meanings. To some Christian Protestant groups the fiddle is "the Devil's instrument," and the names of fiddle tunes and legends certify it: "Devil's Dream," "Devil in the Kitchen," "Devil Went Down to Georgia." The harp, on the other hand, is the instrument of angels. While conservative elements within Islam have condemned many instruments for distracting the faithful, followers of Sufism, who pursue a more mystical interpretation of Islam, often embrace specific instruments in their ritual practices. The

FIGURE 2.8 *Japanese* sankyoku *ensemble. From left to right: Keiko Nosaka* (koto), *Fukami Satomi* (syamisen/shamisen), *Kozan Sato* (syakuhati/shakuhachi). *(Courtesy of Keiko Nosaka)*

Mevlevi Sufis, for example, place the *ney* (flute) in the center of their rituals and philosophy. In the Hindu pantheon the *mṛdaṅgam* drum is associated with Ganesh, the deity of auspicious beginnings, and drummers in South India perform a brief ritual in praise of him to initiate instruction on the instrument. From the offstage instrument room beside the traditional Japanese stage of the *kabuki* theater the deep-sounding strokes of a bell invoke the meditative atmosphere of a Buddhist temple or of impending death (CD track 16), while the chipper combo of flute, drums, and lute invokes the fun of a Shinto shrine festival (CD track 16).

Associations of Gender and Sexuality. Is not B. B. King's guitar named Lucille, and do not instrument teachers sometimes tell pupils to hold the instrument as they would a loved one? The flute of the Hindu god Krishna is playfully suggestive of phallic sexual innuendo, enjoyed by poets and singers and devotees. In Liberia and other places in Africa, drums might be thought of as female.

Ideas about gender sometimes dictate who may and may not play an instrument. In Bulgaria traditionally only men played musical instruments, and the playing of an instrument was an enactment of maleness. Women who played were so exceptional that they were the immediate targets of gossip. In American school music programs, girls are likely to be the flutists, while boys are likely to play percussion, stringed bass, trumpet, and tuba.

In modern global life, gender restrictions in music are decreasing. In China, for example, modern concert traditions are more egalitarian than older ones, and there are many famous female soloists. In recent decades women have been hired to play professionally in symphony orchestras in Europe and the Americas as well.

It can be the performing context that contributes to gender associations, rather than the instrument itself. In Japan, male musicians play *shamisen* (*syamisen*, hereinafter, as per Japanese preference) for *kabuki* and the *bunraku* puppet plays when they are staged, whereas women may play those theatrical repertoires only in concert versions. Men and women equally perform nontheatrical musical genres on *syamisen*, however (figure 2.8).

Cultural Status. Some individual instruments are accorded more prestige than others. Many peoples give primary status to the voice as the best of instruments. In South India vocal music is so dominant that there is no independent instrumental repertoire of compositions; instrumentalists perform songs. The reason for this is clear: the voice is the vehicle for sacred chant (CD track 10), from which Indian music evolved, and music remains primarily a treasured mode for the expression of religious devotion.

In Japan as in Western countries, the piano holds a high status. When European music was adopted there in the process of modernizing the nation in the nineteenth- and early twentieth centuries, the piano was a rare item; only relatively wealthy persons could afford one or had the space to house one. By the time it became widely accessible from Japanese manufacturers such as Yamaha and Kawai, the piano had accrued the prestigious socio-economic associations that it still holds. Americans can understand this easily, thinking of grand pianos that sit unplayed in living rooms as a piece of furniture, transmitting visually the aura of high cultural status.

An instrument's status can be transferred to players and makers of that instrument, so that a sociomusical pecking order develops. In the prestigious Korean court music ensemble the zither-type *komungo* is the

FIGURE 2.9 *Korean* komungo *played by Han Kap-deuk. The* komungo *is a very unusual zither-type instrument in that it has both frets and individual bridges. Its six strings are made of twisted silk. Strings 2, 3, and 4 rest on 16 graduated frets, while strings 1, 5, and 6 are supported by moveable bridges shaped like the foot of a crane. Fine tuning of the strings is executed by round wooden pegs at the bottom of the instrument. The strings are struck with a small bamboo rod.* (Courtesy of the National Center for Korean Traditional Performing Arts)

instrument of highest status (figure 2.9; CD track 17), consequently, until a few years ago, when the present, more democratic system was introduced, the musician who played it held the highest personnel rank. Drums in South India are an interesting case: although the skins of dead animals are considered polluting, drums are considered powerful instruments. Whereas makers of drums, who work with the skins, are of lowest status, players who invoke the power of the instrument are Brahmins, with the highest caste status.

Aesthetic Value. As exhibitions in museums around the world attest, an instrument may be treated as an object of aesthetic value apart from its musical capacity. A drum inlaid with mother-of-pearl, a harpsichord lid embellished with painted flowers and birds, the wooden body of a grand piano gently undulating around a sturdy steel frame—craftsmanship endows these physical objects with artistic beauty.

FIGURE 2.10 *Bamboo xylophones from* gamelan Jegog *of West Bali. Carved on the center* instrument *is Bhoma, fanged protector against evil.* *(Photo by Lisa Gold)*

You can find multiple meanings in the carved case of a bamboo xylophone from *gamelan Jegog* of West Bali (figure 2.10): elaborate embellishment of a valued instrument, yes, but also invocation of Bhoma, son of the forest in the Hindu Balinese pantheon, the fanged protector whose face is often carved over doorways to the inner courtyard in temples and over house doorways to prevent evil from entering.

Item of Technology. Instruments have always been items of technology. It takes only one experience with trying to make one to appreciate the extent to which that is true. However, it took mass production and the burgeoning popularity of electronic instruments to make most of us think of them in technological terms. An average popular music band carts around and sets up an astounding amount of equipment; "the technology" is a member of the band.

People change instruments technologically on a regular basis. For example, the piano did not have even a marginally successful steel frame until about the 1820s. Only after the frame was universally in place, after the middle of the nineteenth century, could thicker and higher-tension strings increase the tonal power, brilliance, and therefore expressive capacity of the piano. Bluhmel added valves for brass instruments in 1818, and Boehm developed a system of mechanical keys for woodwinds in 1832–39. Various durable materials are being used to replace animal skins (i.e., membranes) on drums and strings of natural material on chordophones, and tuning mechanisms have been added to many instruments around the world, from drums to zithers.

No matter how technological a process, the manufacturing of an instrument can become imbued with deep meaning and the maker of an instrument be deemed a person of special cultural significance. The making of gongs in Java and Bali is a spiritually charged craft. Forging a large gong (figure 2.11) is a formidable task, requiring special skills and precise coordination among the members of a team of five or more men. The bronze is unpredictable, and even an experienced team will occasionally fail, having to melt down and reforge. But gongsmiths have long believed that it is a spiritually dangerous task as well, requiring the smith and his men to make particular offerings and take on the names of characters from the medieval Panji legends.

Timbre and Aesthetics of Sound.   Finally, in this discussion of instruments as objects, there is the matter of **timbre**—the quality of the sound of an instrument or voice. "Reedy," "nasal," "growly," "golden": timbres are difficult to describe precisely in words.

It is remarkable how different instruments whose morphology is similar can be made to sound so different. The sound of a basic bamboo flute is modified on the Chinese *di-tze* by placing a paper membrane near the blow hole; the resulting reedy sound can be contrasted with that of the *shakuhachi* without membrane (*syakuhati* hereinafter, as per Japanese preference), for instance (CD track 18, compared with CD track 15).

> ACTIVITY 2.5   *Pick one instrument type that you like to listen to—flute, plucked lute, double reed, or drum, for example. Using the Internet or another source, find at least three greatly contrasting timbres produced on instruments of this type. Explore the reasons why the sounds are so different.*

Perhaps the most meaningful question about timbre brings us to the matter of aesthetics, in this case, values concerning the qualities of mu-

FIGURE 2.11   *Balinese gong.*   *(Photo by Lisa Gold)*

sical sound. In accordance with the sound aesthetics of many African groups, the natural sounds of instruments are likely to be disguised or complemented in some way. In CD track 19, a recording of the Kiembara group of the Senofo (Ivory Coast, West Africa), you can hear several examples of this. The ensemble consists of four xylophones and three bowl-shaped drums of different sizes; rattle-type idiophones attached to the xylophone players' wrists add to the sound. On the xylophones, each wooden bar is resonated by a gourd; each gourd has one or two membranes, which cover specially bored holes to alter the timbre of the sound as they vibrate. The membranes are made from the webs with which certain spiders protect their eggs. In addition, jingles made of pieces of tin and metal rings are fitted to both the smaller kettledrums.

For variety of timbre, perhaps no instrument is more flexible than the human voice. While the variety of timbres produced on chordophones, aerophones, idiophones, and membranophones can be significantly different from instrument to instrument, the variety of timbres that are cultivated by singers around the world is perhaps equalled or surpassed only by sounds created technologically on electronophones. Compare, for example, the aesthetic choice for a beautiful sound in Cantonese opera's female vocal style (CD track 20) and that of European bel canto opera style (CD track 21). Those two examples offer a contrast in the cultivation of nasality as opposed to a clear, open sound.

Consensus about desirable quality of vocal sound is behind exclamations such as "Oh, I don't have a good voice" or "Doesn't she have a wonderful voice!" In the context of Western classical music, those statements are likely to have been made with reference to the European bel canto style. That particular kind of sound is best achieved by focusing on only one portion of a possible vocal **range** (pitch span). The basic ranges from high to low are called **soprano**, **alto**, **tenor**, and **bass**. The expectation that every voice has a naturally comfortable range and that each singer will cultivate and probably expand that range only slightly is a culture-specific idea about the use of the voice. I suggest that it goes hand in hand with the popularity of singing in choruses which give people with different natural comfortable **pitch registers** (area within a pitch range), as well as less "beautiful" voices, an opportunity to make music together.

In other musical traditions the expectation for the pitch range of singers is entirely different. In North Indian (Hindustani) classical music the ideal is to sing in three pitch registers (high, middle, and low), resulting in a range that is considerably wider than most people's "natural voice." I suggest that the requirement for such a wide range is embedded within aesthetic ideas about vocal music: while a singer with a "good voice" according to the Hindustani sound aesthetic will be praised for that, vocalists are more likely to be evaluated for their musical knowledge and improvisatory creativity. Not surprisingly, with single singers taking responsibility for such range, classical vocal music throughout the Indian subcontinent is a solo tradition.

ACTIVITY 2.6 *In your recording collection, find examples of singers you consider to have a "good voice." Try to articulate what the qualities are that make it good. Compare your selection with those of your classmates to see if there is a group consensus about vocal aesthetics.*

INSTRUMENTS IN MUSIC

Put a person together with a musical instrument and a world of possibilities opens up. Such different kinds of music can be made on the same instrument! One need only think of the violin in the hands of a Romanian gypsy musician, a bluegrass fiddler, a Cajun fiddler, an Irish fiddler, a South Indian classical violinist, and a European classical violinist to realize that it is not so much the instrument as human creativity that determines the music's character.

Instrumental Capacity. On the other hand, an instrument must have certain capabilities to meet the expectations of the players or the performing context. Instruments with small sounds (low volume) are appropriate for relatively intimate music making circumstances, and adjustments have to be made if they are to be heard in a large concert hall. Amplification techniques have made a considerable difference there, but some instruments have actually been changed—the piano among them, as European keyboard performance moved from the chamber to the concert hall.

Instruments have their own peculiar characteristics that present the players options that are idiomatic to them. One important physical characteristic is the length of the decay once a sound has been initiated. On some instruments the decay will be relatively rapid, and sustaining a sound means developing a specific technique. It is possible to sustain a pitch on a fiddle with repeated bowing across a string. Singers work on their breath control, as do players of aerophones (particularly those whose instruments have no mechanism for storing air, such as the bladder on a bagpipe). On some instruments a sustained sound is not achievable, so the effect of a sustain is created by other means; on a hammered dulcimer, a xylophone, or a drum, repeated striking will do it. The Peruvian Andean *siku* panpipe provides a good example of achieving a sustained tone both by breath control and cooperative music making (fig. 2–12). In *sikuri* ensemble practice, a melody is played on a pair of instruments, requiring two musicians to interlock their parts (each of

FIGURE 2.12 *Peruvian* sikuri *ensemble in procession.* *(Courtesy of Raul Romero, Center for Andean Ethnomusicology, Catholic University of Peru)*

the first three segments of CD track 22). Within the large circle formation in which *sikuri* ensembles usually play, the paired musicians who interlock parts typically stand next to each other, listening most closely to their partners. Each member of the pair usually holds his note, slightly overlapping with his partner's so that there are no gaps of silence in the melody due to decay of sound (Turino 1993: 44).

Conversely, the long decay of the sound of a gong or a bell must be coped with; one possibility is to assign a sparse musical role to those instruments in an ensemble in order to avoid a muddle of sound, while another possibility is to develop damping techniques. Composers for carillon have a special challenge.

ACTIVITY 2.7 *The beginning moments of Chinese ensemble music on CD track 3 illustrate a sustained pitch played on flute and plucked lute. Once you understand the principle of listening for the different techniques for achieving a sustained pitch, listen to CD track 23, played by a Thai pî phât ensemble (figure 2.13). Try to identify the instrument types. Then listen for the characteristic pattern of decay on each instrument, and how each musician handles the decay in a way that is idiomatic to that instrument.*

Another aspect of the morphology of instruments has been considered by scholars of music cognition: spatial properties, such as the arrangement of slabs or lamellae on an idiophone, relative to the movements that occur in the process of playing that instrument. Several scholars have focused on this spatiality for African musics (von Hornbostel 1928, Blacking 1955, Berliner 1978, Kubik 1979), as have Baily for

FIGURE 2.13   *Thai pî phât ensemble from the Fine Arts Department in Bangkok, Thailand, performing a ritual to honor teachers, 1986. On ranât êk, Natthaphong Sowat, on pî nai, Pip Khonglai Thong. These are some of the best musicians in Central Thailand. From left to right: taphôn, ranât êk, pî nai, ching, ranât thun.*
(Courtesy of Deborah Wong)

Afghani (1985) and Brinner for Javanese (1995) musics. Analyzing tunes played on the Nsenga *kalimba* (thumb piano) and considering the layout of the lamellae relative to the motions of playing, for example, Blacking concluded that "the most significant common factors of the kalimba tunes are not their melodic structures, but the recurring patterns of 'fingering' which, combined with different patterns of polyrhythms between the two thumbs, produce a variety of melodies . . . the tunes are variations on a theme, but the theme is physical and not purely musical" (1961: 6–7). Musical style, then, can be partially a result of the idiomatic morphology of an instrument, and "creativity in music may often consist of deliberately finding new ways to move on an instrument" (Baily 1985: 257).

Ideas about Ensemble.   When musicians play together, the possibilities are infinite. Many factors can obtain, depending on the situation—whether they are jamming or performing formally, or the extent to which they expect to improvise music on the spot as opposed to playing what a composer or arranger provides, or whether a sociomusical hierarchy among the music makers gives one player authority. There is a great deal to listen to and think about with ensemble music making.

A good way to begin listening to music made by a group is to identify the instruments (remembering to include the voice as an instrument). In some performances or compositions or even musical styles the **instrumentation** is clear. As performed by the Dave Brubeck Quartet, for instance, the instrumentation in "Take Five" is clear (CD track 24). Each instrument can be tracked as it enters the performance. The drummer starts the piece, then the pianist comes in. They are joined by the string bass player and finally the sax, in prominent position. The instrumentation of the jazz quartet is nicely balanced, including all of the major categories of instrument types. The drum set incorporates membranophones and an idiophone (high hat cymbal); two chordophones and an aerophone round out the ensemble.

Heterogeneous and Homogeneous Sound Ideals.   This performance of "Take Five" demonstrates both the principles of heterogeneous and homogeneous sound ideals played out in one ensemble. It would be completely heterogeneous (instruments producing clearly different timbres), were it not for the string bass's sounding so similar to the low keys on the piano. Those two sounds are homogeneous.

The **heterogeneous sound ideal**, the love of timbral richness, is widespread. Prominent examples can be found in African music (CD track 19) and in African musics in diaspora—of which jazz is one, of course

FIGURE 2.14 *Japanese* Gagaku *ensemble. From left to right: Front row,* shōko, taiko, kakko; *middle,* kotos, ryūteki, hichiriki, biwas; *rear,* ryūtekis, hichirikis, shōs. *Members of the Tenri University Gagaku Ensemble.* *(Courtesy of Koji Sato)*

(Wilson 1992). It is also enjoyed in Arab music; the ensemble on CD track 25 includes violin, flute, *qanun* (struck board zither) and vocalist. Figure 2.13 explains why the Thai ensemble in CD track 23 presents a heterogeneous sound ideal; some of the instruments are very different from each other.

A second reason why the instrumental parts are clear in "Take Five" is that each instrument enters separately, therefore noticeably. The heterogenous sound ideal and the same principle of bringing in instruments in clear succession occurs in other ensemble music—in the ancient Japanese court music, *gagaku*, for instance (CD track 26; figure 2.14). In the brief prelude in CD track 26, the instruments enter in almost ritualized order; this has become standardized in the approximately thirteen hundred years of the music's existence.

ACTIVITY 2.8 *Listen to the* gagaku *selection (*netori*) on CD track 26. Identify each type of instrument as you hear it enter; here I give you the instrumentarium, but not the order of entry: Stringed (*koto *and* biwa*), flute (*ryūteki*), organlike (*shō*), sharp-sounding drum (*kakko*), and double-reed (*hichiriki*).*

Conversely, the idea of a timbral blend—a **homogeneous sound ideal**—occurs in countless ensembles around the globe, in groups as different as a Polynesian chorus from the Cook Islands (CD track 27) and a brass quintet (CD track 28; figure 2.3). Sometimes, *seeing* the ensemble playing is the only way to *hear* the instruments individually. You might hear Central Javanese *gamelan* music in that way (CD track 8); the homogeneous sound on primarily bronze **metallophones** (pitched metal percussion instrument) and the style of the music create a kind of floating, calm sound. Santosa (2001) writes eloquently about the quality in *gamelan* music desired by villagers with whom he did field research. Listening mostly to radio broadcasts, they sought an atmosphere that evokes the contemplative state: "I want to cite an example in which a middle-aged man claimed that the atmosphere of gamelan performance is similar to that [atmosphere] people want to get when meditating. . . . When conducting meditations he felt *nganyut-nyut*, the state of mind that brought him close to God." It is music meant to hold desire in check. Above all, Santosa found that the *gamelan* tradition is an activity that conserves relations not only among patrons and musicians but also among members of the community; it is a communal practice in which no one individual stands out. Thus the homogeneous sound of the *gamelan* expresses Javanese culture.

The idea of the homogeneous sound ideal is stretched somewhat when an ensemble consists of instruments whose sounds are basically similar but are distinguished by difference in the pitch range—the brass instruments in CD track 28, for instance, and the European bowed lutes from high to low—violin, viola, cello (figure 2.2), and bass.

Dividing a large pitch range among several instruments of the same type occurs in much larger ensembles as well. An instance of this is the Peruvian *sikuri* ensemble, which consists of three (sometimes five) sizes (*cortes*) of the *siku* panpipe (figure 2.12) plus drum, usually the wooden double-headed *bombo* drum. Playing the same melody in multiple pitch registers simultaneously greatly enriches the sound of the ensemble (CD track 22). The first thirty seconds of CD track 22 features the *cortes* called *chili* or *suli* playing a melody of the "Toril" genre, at the highest pitch register of the three sizes of the panpipe demonstrated here. The next thirty seconds gives the same melody played on the middle-register *corte* called *malta*; musicians identify the *malta* as the principal melody carrier of the sizes of *siku* panpipe. The unmistakably lower-register *sanja* is played in a third segment of thirty seconds. For the final portion of CD track 22, all three are featured, entering one by one. For this recorded example an ensemble of twenty to twenty-four performers is pared down to six, two playing interlocking parts on each size of pan-pipe. A large ensemble might even include two more sizes of the instrument (Turino 1993: 41–47).

The practice of dividing a large pitch range among several instruments of the same type ooccurs in a number of ensembles in Southeast Asia, as well. In figure 1.5 you can see two of the three sizes of *saron* in the Central Javanese *gamelan;* the lowest-pitched in the second row has bigger, thicker slabs than the middle-pitched in the foreground. (The highest-pitched is not visible.) Their musical parts are quite different: the higher the register of the instrument, the faster the musical part moves. The performance practice, then, is different from that of the Peruvian *sikuri* ensembles.

One final example brings into play all three ideas I have presented thus far about ensemble: timbral mix, multiple sizes of similar instruments, and highlighting of selected instruments. The sound of the mariachi ensemble combines both homogeneity and heterogeneity. The large *guitarrón* (bass guitar) and the much smaller *vihuela* (rhythm guitar) are strikingly similar in shape and arguably reflect the European Renaissance ideal of blended sound (figure 2.15). When combined with the vi-

FIGURE 2.15 *Principal instruments of a Mexican mariachi ensemble. From left to right:* vihuela, *Armando Quintero;* guitarrón, *Francisco "El Capiro" Castro;* violin, *Hilario Cervantes;* trumpet, *Luis "El Loco" Pérez.* *(Courtesy of Daniel Sheehy)*

olin, as was often the case before the 1940s, the ensemble sound was still relatively homogeneous. The latter half of the twentieth century saw the addition of the trumpet, creating a mariachi sound purposefully marked by timbral contrast and dynamism. The contrast is marked in CD track 29, as the trumpeter enters after we have settled into the sound of the strings.

ACTIVITY 2.9 *Pick out three of your favorite musical performing groups and think about the instrumentation. Do the instruments contribute to a homogeneous or heterogeneous sound ideal, or a bit of both?*

Musical Roles. An additional way to think about ensembles is to consider the nature of the musical roles taken by the musicians. In an ensemble making North Indian classical music, three musical roles will be filled: someone plays a melody-producing instrument, someone maintains a basic pitch reference (a drone), and someone plays a percussion instrument. Similarly, in New Orleans jazz a "front line" of instruments collectively improvises on the melody while a second line plays the fixed rhythmic background.

The words **solo** and **accompaniment** delineate musical roles. "Soloist" is a somewhat confusing word, since on the one hand it means someone who makes music totally alone and on the other refers to a person in an ensemble whose music is meant to stand out most prominently—like the opera singer on CD track 21 and the North Indian singer on CD track 30. We are likely to assume that a musical hierarchy is at work, with the "soloist" more important than the "accompanist(s)." Beware of that, however! In musical styles like jazz (CD track 24 "Take Five") and North Indian instrumental genres the "soloist" role might pass from music maker to music maker, so the role of "accompanist" shifts too.

The words "conductor" and "leader" and "master" also name musical roles. In some performance traditions, a leader is visually obvious: the conductor of a Western orchestra, for example. In both the Central Javanese *gamelan* (CD track 8) and some Chinese ensembles, however, a drummer leads the timing of the performance; he sends musical signals by drumming patterns that are embedded in the fabric of the music. There are, then, both highly visible and clearly audible types of "con-

FIGURE 2.16 *West African Music Ensemble. C. K. Ladzekpo, master drummer. Front row, left to right: Val Kai (dancer); C. K. Ladzekpo, standing (playing At-simevu [lead drum]); Trevino Leon, sitting (playing* gangokui *[bell]); Moddy Perry, sitting (playing* Sogo *[drum]). Back row, left to right: Kokou Kadamani (playing* gangokui *[bell]); Joni Hastrup.* (Photo by Kathleen Karn)

ductor." The master drummer in an African musical ensemble is both visible and audible; he is the one musician who is free to improvise, and he signals through drumming when the other musicians should change their musical parts (figure 2.16; CD track 5).

Musical roles in ensembles may be taken by persons other than per-formers. In Trinidadian steelbands (CD track 2), an arranger makes mu-sical decisions, assuming a leadership role that in earlier days was ac-corded to those who were able to make the instruments—the tuners—because it was not possible to buy them from someone else. They work with section leaders of subgroups in the ensemble who are appointed for their playing skills.

Perhaps the most important ideal for an ensemble is the way the mu-sicians interact during performance, the way they contribute to en-hancing not only the overall sound of the group but also the silence: Balinese *gamelan* music exploits sudden starts and stops, requiring split-second coordination as silence as well as sound is used to dramatic effect (CD track 31). For a Balinese musician, the ultimate goal is to contribute to a sense of oneness with a group of musicians, whether the group is a duo or a forty-five-member ensemble. This oneness results from years of training and practicing together, working toward the ultimate aesthetic of tight precision, called *kompak* ("compact") or *sip* ("tight"). Balinese music is a deeply communal practice.

In this chapter I have considered several ways of thinking about instruments. As objects they have been classified in different ways in different cultures, have accrued extra-musical associations, and expressed aesthetic values both visually and in terms of sound quality. Interrelationships among musicians, their instruments, and the music they make were explored through ideas about ensemble. In the next chapter I turn my attention to the organization of musical time, focusing first on rhythm, then on speed.

CHAPTER 3

Thinking about Time

∞

In this chapter I explore the ways in which musicians organize time in music. Except when there is a constant drone, there is always **rhythm** in musical sound, created by successions of durations. In a context filled with sound, the absence of sound (i.e., silence) becomes significant as well. A consistent set of terms is used in talking about time in music, including "rhythm," "pulse," "beat," "count," "feel," "groove," "rhythmic mode," "meter," and others.

ACTIVITY 3.1 *Conduct this mini-fieldwork project with at least five of your friends. (1) Before you read further, write definitions of these terms: "pulse," "beat," "count," "feel," "groove," "rhythm," "meter." (2) Ask your friends to define the terms. (3) Play for each friend a musical piece of your choice and ask each separately to talk about it using those words. If they use other words to describe time in the music, keep track of them. You will emerge with a sense of your and their perceptions about the flow of musical sound. Where is there consensus, and where is there difference among the definitions?*

In coordinating the definitions of terms as authors are using them in the case studies in this Global Music Series, I found the greatest differences in the way we understand the practices encompassed by terms pertinent to the organization of time. That is because concepts of musical time differ greatly in different traditions. Our teachers have explained the ideas in their own ways, and we ethnomusicologists assume the task of translating them. In so doing, we draw on a vocabulary that is small because relatively little attention has been paid to time in European art music—the source of most musical terminology in English-language writing. This has caused single words to have multiple meanings; the term "meter," for instance, is applied to qualitatively different concepts about the organization of musical time. The implications of the words "rhythm" as opposed to "meter" and "pulse" as opposed to "beat" are particularly confusing.

RHYTHM

It is useful to distinguish between **rhythm** in general and "a rhythm." By "rhythm" I mean the aspect of music having to do with the duration of pitches in time—any succession of durations. "A rhythm," in contrast, is a specific succession of durations.

Pulse. More often than not, musicians organize rhythm in some purposeful fashion. Rhythm in dance music, for example, or in rap, is very purposefully organized. Whether you call the steady, equal-length durations that organize rap "pulse" or "beat" or something else, it is clear that organizing time is a defining characteristic of the rap style. Enunciating steady, equal-lengthed durations is a basic unit in music with organized time. I call this **pulse,** comparing it to the heartbeat; calling it **beat** is common too.

A good way to focus on the organization of time in music is to try to feel a pulse—steady, equal-length durations that are somehow enunciated musically. It helps to move with the music—nod your head, pat your foot, clap your hands, tap a finger discreetly, get up and dance. Move! In giving this direction to move, I acknowledge that growing up dancing or embodying a sense of rhythm in some other way is not in everyone's experience. In some cultures young people are taught to move their bodies as little as possible; whatever the reason—gender, class, religious belief—that can affect their perception and practice of rhythm. So I recommend strongly that you do a lot of beat-keeping to music when you listen, even if it is a mental rather than physical exercise.

ACTIVITY 3.2 *Play some of your favorite music and, as you listen, express the pulse you feel. For variety, you might try feeling regular durations in some of the music on this book's CD. Do not try to count anything; just feel the pulse.*

Irregular Durations. On the other hand, musicians sometimes purposefully leave rhythm unorganized, that is, with little or no sense of predictability about the organization of time. This could be due to the expectations for a musical genre or perhaps an individual composer's will. Musicians might be at liberty to let the rhythm be freely flowing, and scholars speak of the resulting music in various ways: as being in free rhythm or **nonmetrical**, as *(parlando) rubato* or pulseless free flow in time. Such a rhythmic style occurs in many musical practices around the world. In some instances, it is a structural principle, an expected way of beginning a musical piece. On CD track 8, Central Javanese *gamelan* music, the first eleven seconds are free rhythmically, though convention constrains the solo player to a certain extent. On CD track 11, a brief excerpt at the beginning of a selection of North Indian *sitār* music, the musician is expected in the style to improvise in free rhythm. On CD track 23, an entire Thai *pî phât* ensemble plays nonmetrical rhythm (not organized in regular units) to initiate a piece. Louis Armstrong chose to begin "West End Blues" (CD track 32) with a trumpet solo in free rhythm.

Extending this principle, in much Japanese *syakuhati* music the rhythm of an entire selection (beyond an excerpt such as that on CD track 15) is nonmetrical, sustaining a meditative mood. The music is precomposed to be that way, as is the nonmetrical beginning of CD track 25, Egyptian ensemble music. The selection on CD track 25 is the instrumental introduction (**muqaddima**) and beginning of a song performed by the legendary Umm Kulthum. Scott Marcus refers to this initial ensemble section as "the *rubato* section," in *parlando rubato.*

Coordinating through "breathing rhythm," the members of the conductorless Japanese *gagaku* ensemble introduce the melodic mode of the selection they are about to play with an introductory preludelike *netori.* Trying to find regular durations through CD track 26 is fruitless; breathing with it is a more appropriate idea.

ACTIVITY 3.3 *Pick up whatever object you have at hand to use as a percussion instrument and play with creating rhythm that is first regular, then free, then regular, then free. This will help you embody these two different senses of rhythm in time.*

Rhythm for the Text Alone. In some music the rhythm is the servant of the text. **Recitative** in Western opera is one example of this. As its name implies, recitative is singing that imitates and emphasizes in both rhythm and pitch the natural flow of speech. Although the melody has been precomposed, an opera singer can have fun with the rhythm as Carmen does in her four-line response to the soldiers who are anxious for her attention: "When will I love you? Really, I don't know. Perhaps never, perhaps tomorrow. But not today. That's certain!" (CD track 21, from 0:32 to 1:01).

Traditions of religious chant exist for the purpose of rendering sacred texts, so the rhythmic setting of the text is of particular concern. On CD track 1, moments of recitation of the second chapter (*sura*) of the Koran, express these words: "In the Name of God, the Merciful, the Compassionate." Not only these devotees of the Qadiriya Sufi brotherhood in Turkey but all Muslims everywhere adhere to rules for the rhythm that were established to elucidate the text when reciting the sacred text revealed to the Prophet Muhammad.

ORGANIZING TIME INTO UNITS

In most of the world's music, musicians organize time into units longer than one pulse/beat/count. Terms for the different sorts of units are "meter," "rhythmic mode," "*clave*," and such. The basic defining feature of units of organized time is some total number of counts. The quantity can be anything—from two-beat *samba* meter to a South Indian *tāla* cycle of 128 counts. In each case the unit functions to mark off musical flow through time.

Beyond the number of counts, exploring what defines a unit in various musical systems becomes complex and fascinating. In the rest of this chapter I provide examples of different sorts of units—meters of several varieties, rhythmic modes, colotomic structure, and others. First, I present a group of meters that may be articulated in music in any number of ways—harmonically, melodically, percussively, or by bodily motions. Then I will discuss types of organization of time whose musical articulation in performance is dictated.

Duple and Triple Meters. The simplest meters have two or three counts; the former is called "duple," the latter is called "triple." Each unit of two or three counts constitutes a **measure** or **bar**, terminology from Western music notation, which puts vertical bars (measure bars) between units (see figure 1.11).

Meter is usually defined as a pattern of strong and weak counts. That definition works well when the pattern is played out musically (articulated) with clear accentuation so that it can be felt. In "Marieke" (CD track 33), most often associated with the late Belgian poet, songwriter, and cabaret performer Jacques Brel, the triple meter is articulated clearly in the bass with a primary stress on 1 but a secondary stress on 3 that anticipates the next count 1. In addition, **waltzes** are in triple meter; if you have danced a waltz, you have already embodied the feeling of it.

The stress pattern of triple meter (and other meters) is not always so clearly performed, however. Whether or not to articulate the pattern clearly is a musical option. CD track 34, the Waltz in C-sharp Minor by the Polish composer Frédéric Chopin (1810–49), is a waltz meant for concert presentation. Its speed is too fast for dancing and also there is considerable ebb and flow in the pace of the counts, as appropriate in the *rubato* performing style. If you were to listen to the entire piece, you would notice moments when the triple meter is hard to feel because it is not being articulated by musical stresses; it is still there however—in theory.

Meters with multiples of two counts are also considered to be duple meters—units of four counts, for instance: **1** 2 3 4 | **1** 2 3 4 |. It is common for a four-count unit to feel like it comprises subunits (2 + 2), owing to stress being put on count 3 in addition to the expected strong stress placed on count 1 (the **downbeat**): | ♪ • ♪ • | ♪ • ♪ • |.

ACTIVITY 3.4 *Listen to CD track 6, "Calypso Freedom," in a meter of four counts: 1 2 3 4 | 1 2 3 4 |. Listen also to "West End Blues," past the beginning trumpet solo; in the first chorus the pianist clearly articulates the counts (CD track 32). Each chorus is twelve measures long; this is a perfect example of what is known as "twelve-bar blues," with each bar being four counts long.*

Do you feel the four counts in a bar being performed as 2 + 2?

Duple meter offers a good context for introducing the principle of rhythmic **syncopation**. (With syncopation, the word "beat" is more usual than "count" or "pulse.") Once a regular beat is firmly established, rhythmic interest can be added by putting an accent in an unexpected place. If you count 1 AND 2 AND 3 AND 4 AND, stressing the AND, you have got the sense of "offbeat" syncopation. Another type of syncopation consists of accenting a beat where stress is not expected: If, in a regular grouping of four counts, you put stress on the "weak" counts 2 and 4 rather than the "strong" counts 1 and 3, that is a kind of syncopation sometimes called a "backbeat." If, as in CD track 35, the backbeat stress continues for very long, you can lose the sense of the "regular" beat. What defines the offbeat as offbeat is the framework that locates the strong "on" beat; because of that, syncopated music commonly combines strong downbeats with offbeat and backbeat stresses. Syncopation is a basic ingredient in African and African diaspora musics, but it occurs in many other musical traditions as well.

ACTIVITY 3.5   *To challenge your hearing of triple and duple meters, listen to CD track 36, Dave Brubeck's "Three to Get Ready and Four to Go," until you find it easy to count out the measures.*

The piece begins entirely in triple measures, with four phrases of three measures each, for a total of twelve measures. The piano gives the melody, while the bass plays on each count 1. Listen for the high hat (cymbal in the drum set) being struck offbeat, on count 2.

Phrase 1: 1 2 3 | 1 2 3 | 1 2 3 |
Phrase 2: 1 2 3 | 1 2 3 | 1 2 3 |
Phrase 3: 1 2 3 | 1 2 3 | 1 2 3 |
Phrase 4: 1 2 3 | 1 2 3 | 1 2 3 |

For the second chorus (from 0:12) the alto sax takes the melody. The metric pattern changes to phrases of two measures of triple plus two measures of duple (4) from that point to the end.

Phrase 1: 1 2 3 | 1 2 3 | 1 2 3 4 | 1 2 3 4 |
Phrase 2: 1 2 3 | 1 2 3 | 1 2 3 4 | 1 2 3 4 |
Phrase 3: 1 2 3 | 1 2 3 | 1 2 3 4 | 1 2 3 4 |
Phrase 4: 1 2 3 | 1 2 3 | 1 2 3 4 | 1 2 3 4 |

If you can count the pattern easily, you are very secure with duple and triple meter. If so, listen for another detail: It is in the duple measures that the instrumentalists take brief solos and play around.

Simple and Compound Meters. In exploring syncopation, we divided each beat into two equal parts by counting "1 and 2 and 3 and 4 and." Meters that divide each count or beat into two parts this way are called **simple meters**; simple meters may be triple or duple, as already shown.

Compound meters divide each beat or count into *three* equal divisions. Again, the number of beats in each measure may be a multiple of two (duple) or three (triple). A compound duple meter, then, looks as follows:

Subunit: • • • • • •
Beat: • •

In CD track 37, the Irish **jigs** "Tar Road to Sligo" (beginning to 1:31) and "Paddy Clancy's" (from 1:32) are both in compound duple meter, as shown with dots above. The beats are stressed musically in performance, so you should be able to feel them; saying "jiggity, jiggity" along with the music may help you feel the division. (A variant of the Irish jig not illustrated on the CD is the **slip jig**, in compound triple meter: three beats per measure, each divided into three parts.)

Additive Meters. When the total number of pulses in a measure is a number such as 5, 7, or 11, rather than a multiple of 2 or 3, the meter is likely to be called **additive meter**. Within each measure, the pulses tend to form asymmetrical groups or subunits—3 + 2, 2 + 2 + 3, and so forth. This organization of time occurs in many musics, in jazz and in Russian and Balkan dances, for example.

In Paul Desmond's "Take Five"—a composition whose title gives away the total number of pulses in each measure—the meter is 3 + 2 (CD track 24). It is there in the initial drum introduction, but the Dave Brubeck Quartet performs it clearly when the piano and bass come in with a pitch pattern (pitches 1 and 5, see chapter 4) that articulates the subunits.

```
Counts:  1  2  3  4  5  |  1  2  3  4  5  |  1  2  3  4  5  |
Pitches: 1  •  •  5  •  |  1  •  •  5  •  |  1  •  •  5  •  |
```

The bass player is given the musical role of keeping the metric pattern through most of the piece, with that recurring 1–5 pitch pattern. It is reinforced by chord changes, at times on the piano. (Pitch—including chords—is explained in chapter 4).

In his volume in this series, Tim Rice translates the principle behind Bulgarian additive meters using the word "count" to describe the basic pulse and the word "beat" to describe the grouping of pulses within the measure. In a five-count meter, a measure has five counts but only two beats, of unequal length: long (three counts) and short (two counts). Similarly, a measure of seven counts with subunits of 3 + 2 + 2 is perceived as having three beats in the pattern long = short = short:

```
Counts:   1   2   3   4   5   6   7   |
          •   •   •   •   •   •   •   |
Beats:    long        short short   |
          3 +         2 +   2        |
```

This is the meter on CD track 38, a melody for the *makedonsko horo* dance, played on a *tambura* (plucked lute). It is articulated by bowing on the drone pitches.

ACTIVITY 3.6 *To help you hear the additive meters in both the jazz piece "Take Five" (CD track 24) and the Bulgarian makedonsko horo (CD track 38), practice them first without listening. Clap on the stressed counts while speaking the counts: For the 5: Clap on 1 and 4.*
For the 7: Clap on 1, 4, and 6.
Since it is a bit awkward to count from 1 to 7 at the fast speed of the recording, try speaking it as
1 2 3 1 2 1 2 | 1 2 3 1 2 1 2 | 1 2 3 1 2 1 2 |, as Tim Rice does on the recording to get you started.

  After a while, keep clapping but stop speaking the counts. Let yourself feel the short and long subgroups with a kind of swing.

Then put on the recordings and listen again. Figure 3.1 is a partial transcription of the makedonsko horo; *it might help you hear the meter.*

South Indian Tāla.   South Indian *tāla* (meter) shares with compound meter and additive meter the importance of the quality of the subunits. The subunits (*anga*) may all contain the same number of counts, or they may be uneven. There are three types of subunit: a 1-count subunit, a 2-count subunit, and a subunit that can have either 3, 4, 5, 7, or 9 counts (or, as Karnatak musicians order them, 4, 3, 7, 5, 9, for a reason explained in Allen and Vishwanathan's volume on South India in this series). Most Karnatak *tāla*s consist of particular combinations of those types. The total number of counts in a *tāla* structure, then, depends on the number of counts called for in the subunits. The *tāla* most frequently drawn on for compositions is *ādi tāla*; its eight-count grouping is 4 + 2 + 2 (CD track 39)—subunits of four, two, and two counts, respectively.

ACTIVITY 3.7   *On CD track 39, T. Vishwanathan sings a portion of a song, clapping out* ādi tāla *so that you can hear the strongest counts. Count it out as you listen. The first line of text is repeated several times, and you can get the* tāla *from it. Count 1 of the* tāla *falls on "Un" of "unnai."*

Count	1	2	3	4	5	6	7	8	
Subunit	4			2		2			
Count placement	•	•	•	•	•	•	•	•	
Text		Unnai nambinen ayya caranam, nan							
		"I worshiped you, lord, I prostrated at your feet."							

All of the types of meters discussed thus far—triple and duple, simple and compound, additive and South Indian *tāla*—have this in common: When time in the music being performed is organized by one of them, the musicians have options for how they might make listeners aware of the structures. Musicians can choose to mask the meter, or they can draw on one or more means—melody, harmony, instrumentation,

Original pitch: B

FIGURE 3.1 *Bulgarian* makedonsko horo. Performed by Tsvetanka Varimezova. *(Transcription by Angela Rodel)*

drum pattern, dance pattern, hand clapping, or something else—to articulate it. *How the meter is performed is not part of what defines the meter.*

Now I move to structures in which a particular performance practice is an essential part of what defines the system for organizing musical time. Including meter but exceeding it, this encompasses such systems as colotomic structure, rhythmic mode, and African polyrhythm.

Southeast Asian Colotomic Structure. A clear example of an essential performance practice that articulates the metric structure is found in most Southeast Asian ensemble music: **colotomic structure**, in which one or more instruments in an ensemble is consistently assigned the musical role of articulating the metric structure. In Central Javanese *gamelan* music, the instruments assigned to do this are pitched gongs.

In the *gamelan* music of Central Java, the number of counts in a metric unit will be duple—8 or 16 or 32 or 64, and so forth. Interestingly, the *last* count of a grouping—count 8 or 16, for instance—is the most significant count. That beat is clearly marked by a stroke on the largest gong (*ageng*) in the ensemble; it literally holds together the metric structure.

ACTIVITY 3.8 *Feeling the last count as the point of greatest emphasis requires considerable reorientation for those of us accustomed to place the stress on count 1. Without listening to music, count out cycles of eight beats, giving greatest weight to the eighth beat by saying the word "GONG" in deep tones. If you do this while walking, you will get the sense of it quite easily. Also, putting a slight stress on beats 2, 4, and 6 as points of arrival will help you feel the approach of that important last count in the cycle. Do this until it feels right for the cycle to culminate in count 8.*

The complete colotomic structure is as follows:

- The *gong ageng* (G) marks off the whole cycle (called a *gongan*).
  - • The *kenong* (N), a large kettle gong, subdivides the *gongan* into two *kenongan*: the *kempul* (P), a hanging gong, marks the midpoint of the seond *kenongan*.
    - • • The *kempul* (P) and *kethuk* (t), two hanging gongs, subdivide the *kenongan*.

Because this same pattern is played over and over again through a musical composition, it is considered to be cyclical. The pattern of strokes for a sixteen-count cycle is shown here, with letters indicating which instrument plays at that point. The last count (here 16, but in Activity 3.8, count 8) functions as both a beginning and ending count, so the structure is cyclical in two senses of the word.

```
      16 | 1  2  3  4  5  6  7  8  9  10 11 12 13 14 15 16 |
•      G                                                  G
••     N              •        N           P              N
•••         p  t  p      p  t  p     p  t  p     p  t  p
```

Collapsed into a single line, you can easily see that the only count on which there is no stroke in the colotomic structure is count 4; a **rest** occurs there. The only count where two strokes coincide is the last count of the cycle, stressing its structural significance. A piece will end with a stroke on the *gong ageng* that is a little delayed, for climactic finality.

```
16 | 1  2  3  4  5  6  7  8  9  10 11 12 13 14 15 16 |
G     p  t  p  •  p  t  p  N  p  t  p  P  p  t  p  G
```

ACTIVITY 3.9 *Speak the Central Javanese gamelan colotomic structure, saying "gong" for G, "nong" for N, "tuk" (as in "took") for t, "pul" (as in "pool") for P. You will feel the interlocking nature of it if you do it with friends, dividing the instrumental parts among you.*

When you have the flow of it, including the stress pattern, listen to CD track 8, "Ketawang Puspawarna," a composition with that metric cycle of sixteen counts. You should recognize the beginning from listening to this selection before: the short nonmetrical passage played on the rebab *(bowed lute). The drummer enters soon, and melodic pitches played on a metallophone next.*

0:14 The first GONG *stroke. From this point it will take a complete cycle through the structure for the speed of the counts to settle down, and you may not be able to feel the beat yet. But try.*

1:01 The second GONG stroke. From here you should be able to count; each beat takes about two seconds.
1:29 The third GONG stroke
1:57 The fourth GONG stroke

Because the gongs that perform the colotomic structure are playing pitches in the melody, the marking of the important counts is greatly submerged in the ensemble sound. If you were sitting in the ensemble, however, you would be consciously listening to or automatically hearing them. This is discussed further in Benjamin Brinner's volume on Java in this series.

North Indian Tāla.   North Indian *tāla* is another example of a metric system in which a given means of articulation is part of what defines a particular meter. Two North Indian *tāla*s with the same number of total counts and the same subunit structure will be distinguished by a way they are articulated on the drum—through a one-cycle-long stroking pattern (a brief composition, really) called *theka.*

For example, the *tāla* with a twelve-count cycle, with subunits of 2 + 2 + 2 + 2 + 2 + 2 and articulated on the *pakhāwaj* (a modified barrel-shaped, double-headed drum) is a meter called *chautāl.* A *tāla* with a twelve-count cycle, with the same subunit structure, but articulated on the *tablā* (drum pair) is *ektāl.* Furthermore, two *tāla*s with the same structure played on the same drum—*tīntāl* and *tilwāḍā tāla,* each sixteen counts (4 + 4 + 4 + 4) played on *tablā,* for instance—are distinguished partially by the *theka* through which they are articulated. (*Tilwāḍā* is used for slow selections, while *tīntāl* is used for any speed.) A Hindustani musician, if asked to demonstrate a particular *tāla* will speak the *theka,* using syllables to indicate the strokes that would be played on the drum. The syllables have some relationship (though sometimes not much) to the sound that the stroke will produce on the drum.

ACTIVITY 3.10 *Speak these North Indian* theka*s, as they are taught by Pandit Swapan Chaudhuri. Underlining indicates multiple syllables spoken in one count. Compare the rhythmic* *feel and sounds of the drumming strokes in* chautāl *and* ektāl theka, *then the* tīntāl *and* tilwāḍā theka*s*.

The tāla *cycle is also kept physically, with claps and waves of the hand. Once you have the feel of the spoken patterns of the* thekas, *try to speak them while keeping the* tāla. *A* + *indicates count 1; clap when you speak the syllable. Other numbers indicate counts where you should clap as well. On counts marked with 0, wave your hand.*

Chautāl (played on pakhāwaj*) 2 + 2 + 2 + 2 + 2 + 2*

+	0	2	0	3	4

dha dha | *dhin ta* | *kat <u>dhage</u>* | *dhin ta* | *<u>tete</u> <u>kate</u>* | *<u>gadhi</u> <u>gene</u>*

Ektāl (played on tablā*) 2 + 2 + 2 + 2 + 2 + 2*

+	0	2	0	3	4

dhin dhin | *<u>dhage</u> <u>tete</u>* | *tun na* | *kat ta* | *<u>dhage</u> <u>tete</u>* | *dhin <u>dhage</u>*

Tīntāl (played on tablā*) 4 + 4 + 4 + 4*

+	2	0	3

dha dhin dhin dha| *dha dhin dhin dha* |*na tin tin ta* |*ta dhin dhin dha*

Tilwāḍā (played on tablā*) 4 + 4 + 4 + 4*

+	2

Dha -<u>kra</u> dhin dhin | *dha dha tin <u>terekita</u>* |

0	3

ta -<u>kra</u> dhin dhin | *dha dha dhin <u>terekita</u>*

Middle Eastern Rhythmic Modes. The Arabic term *iqá* (*usul* in Turkish) is usually translated as "rhythmic mode" rather than "meter," suggesting the qualitative nature of the rhythmic aspect of traditional Arab and Turkish music. A **rhythmic mode** is a metric structure that also bears particular expressive qualities. (Mode, as related to mood, I discuss in chapter 4.)

So many rhythmic modes have the same total number of counts that distinguishing them quantitatively makes no sense. Instead, each rhythmic mode is defined by the way it is articulated, that is, performed on a drum. (You can see in this how Hindustani drumming was influenced by the concepts and practices taken to North India by immigrant musicians from West Asia over a period of several hundred years, climaxing in the seventeenth century.)

In the Middle East there is a great variety of drums, each capable of producing a variety of sounds. Only two sounds, however, *dumm* and *takk* (Arabic language) are used to define the individual rhythmic modes. *Dumm* is the deepest or lowest sound the instrument can produce. *Takk* is high-pitched, the sound produced when striking where the head meets the rim of the drum.

Each rhythmic mode is defined by a unique skeletal pattern of *dumm*s and *takk*s. Comparison of three different eight-count rhythmic modes should make this point clear: D indicates *dumm*, T indicates *takk*, and a dash (−) indicates a rest. The names of the modes here are those used in the eastern Arab world; they are called by different names in different places.

Count	1	2	3	4	5	6	7	8
Maqsum	D	T	−	T	D	−	T	−
Masmudi saghir	D	D	−	T	D	−	T	−
Sáidi	D	D	−	D	D	−	T	−

ACTIVITY 3.11 *Speak the patterns of the Middle Eastern rhythmic modes, making deep and high (heavy and light) sounds for* dumm *and* takk. *Do this at several speeds and you will feel the relative weighting of the mode caused by the defining strokes.*

Now listen to CD track 25. You are familiar with the non-metrical rubato *section that begins the ensemble introduction (*muqaddima*) to the song that will follow. The* rubato *section extends to 1:27, encompassing a beginning by full ensemble, followed by interaction between a soloist on* qanun *(frame zither) and the ensemble response. The next section of the introduction, starting at 1:28, is measured—in* maqsum *rhythmic mode. Listen particularly for the* riqq *(tambourine with jingling cymbals in the frame).*

In performing music in a rhythmic mode, drummers can make some substitutions or embellishments to the patterns in the interest of timbral and expressive variety, but the mode's defining weighting needs to be maintained. The extent of the embellishment should tastefully reflect the overall context in which the rhythm occurs—little, perhaps, when accompanying a slowly moving section of a lyrical song, and much, perhaps, when accompanying a rousing dance. Options, too, are part of what makes rhythmic mode qualitative.

Korean Changdan. Korean **changdan** are in some ways similar to Middle Eastern rhythmic modes. *Changdan* are rhythmic patterns that are drummed or in some other way articulated in musical performance: "a series of accented and unaccented strokes or beats" (Hesselink 1996: 152). Unlike any other time-organizing units I have presented here, some of the rhythmic patterns (*changdan*) occur in nonmetrical music and others in metered contexts.

The rhythmic patterns vary in length (total number of counts), but the number of counts in a unit is not emphasized as a particularly important distinguishing trait of a *changdan*. In this, the unit is more appropriately called a "grouping" than a "meter" (Lerdahl and Jackendoff 1981).

Two other defining characteristics of *changdan* are new in this discussion of time. One is speed; *changdan* are performed at specified (though relative) speeds. (Speed is of some consideration in Middle Eastern and North Indian *talas* but takes relatively less of a defining role there than in *changdan*.) Secondly, the amount of repetition of a particular *changdan* that can occur in a musical selection is another defining trait—free repetition or a set number of repetitions, for example. This extremely elaborate system for the organization of time indicates the importance of rhythm in Korean traditional music: most Korean ensembles, like Middle Eastern and Indian ensembles, include a percussionist.

Within a *changdan* drumming pattern an aesthetic sense of tension and release should be discernible. *Kutkori changdan*, for instance, is a pattern of twelve counts in slow speed. The feel of the pattern is of four groups of three counts each. Drummed on the double-headed hourglass-shaped drum *chang-gu* (figure 3.2), you can feel gathering intensity from the first six beats, climaxing during beats 7–9, and letting down during the last three beats.

ACTIVITY 3.12 *To feel the triple rhythm of* kutkori *chang-dan, first count* **1 2 3** *slowly several times. Korean musicians think of it as a rhythmic pulse based on breath (*hohup*), so you think the counts as you exhale on* **1** *and inhale on* **2** *and* **3**. *Continue to think* **1 2 3** *slowly.*

FIGURE 3.2 *Korean percussion ensemble. From left to right: Peter Kim (*puk drum*), Eunyang Kwon (*jing gong*), Patrick Chew (*chang-gu drum*), Donee Lee (*ggwaengwari gong*). (Courtesy of Donna Kwon)*

> Now bend your knees so that you drop down slightly on *1* and rise slowly on *2 and 3*. This is ogum, *deep up-and-down movement of the body, coordinated with breathing. Do this exercise again several times, counting from 1 to 12 but keeping up the triple pattern. In this way you will feel the whole length of* kutkori changdan.
>
> *Now speak the syllables for the strokes on the* chang-gu, *proceeding through the* kutkori *pattern to feel the sense of the aesthetic cycle.*
>
> | 1 | 2 | 3 | 4 | 5 | 6 | 7 | 8 | 9 | 10 | 11 | 12 |
> |---|---|---|---|---|---|---|---|---|----|----|----|
> | Dong | | dak | Kung | [da da] | dak | Kung | | dak | Kung | dak | |
>
> Dong *indicates hitting both heads at the same time.*

Dak *indicates hitting the right head with a thin, flat stick.*
Da *is a lighter version of* dak, *hitting with just the tip rather than the flat part of the stick;* [ ] *indicates filler strokes.*
Kung *indicates hitting left or right head with a wooden mallet. (Exercise courtesy of Donna Kwon)*

As in Middle Eastern and Hindustani drumming, the drumming patterns that articulate Korean rhythmic units can be varied in performance. The extent and the ways in which a drummer can do that, of course, are learned within each tradition.

African Polyrhythm. Polyrhythm as a defining musical trait is a gift of African music makers to musicians throughout the world. **Polyrhythm** is the musical texture of performing multiple rhythmic patterns simultaneously. In much African ensemble music south of the Sahara desert, different instruments have their own rhythmic patterns that are repeated many times, in effect multiple rhythmic ostinatos. (An **ostinato** is a constantly recurring motive.) Each rhythmic pattern functions to mark off time spans in the musical flow. The patterns are not to be thought of in terms of meter, however: each is a grouping of beats without metrical accent.

One of two primary structuring principles of polyrhythmic music is the interacting and coordinating of all the different patterns, and those often coordinating with dance as well. Two elements hold it all together.

One coordinating element is a timeline of pulses—steady, equidistant sounds, a reference point for the passage of time. Some instrumentalist is usually designated the role of articulating that timeline. In her volume on West Africa in this series, Ruth Stone writes about the well-known Nigerian timeline of twelve pulses.

The second coordinating element is a rhythmic pattern played on a double metal bell; the timbre of the bell is easily distinguishable from other instruments and thus can be clearly heard. Here I cite a bell pattern of which Stone also speaks in her volume; it functions within the twelve-pulse timeline, marking off beats as follows: 2 + 2 + 3 + 2 + 3. "Beat" here is analogous to the "beat" in Bulgarian music, with durations of different length. The pattern is spoken with **mnemonic** syllables.

Pulse:	•	•	•	•	•	•	•	•	•	•	•	•
Syllables:	Kong		kong		ko – lo			kong		ko – lo		
Beat:	2		2		3			2		3		

In ensemble practice, all the other musicians coordinate with the bell pattern and with each other, using the underlying pulse as a reference point. In performance, most of the musicians will repeat their pattern until cued to switch; the performers whose pattern remains constant are the players of the timeline and the double metal bell. In his volume on Trinidad in this series, Shannon Dudley defines this rhythmic texture as featuring "a constant rhythmic feel or 'groove' that is created by the interaction of repeating and contrasting parts."

The second primary structuring principle in this African polyrhythmic music is that "contrasting part" mentioned by Dudley. In many African ensembles one individual is free to improvise; that person is likely to be the most prestigious musician. In drumming ensembles, that would be the master drummer (figure 2.16). He (it is usually a man) is in charge; he will signal the other musicians when to switch rhythmic patterns in the course of playing. His organization of time through improvised rhythmic patterns is relatively freer than that of the other musicians, but he, too, feels that underlying pulse and interacts with the multiple ostinatos, including the bell pattern.

ACTIVITY 3.13 *The Ghanaian example on CD track 5 is an excerpt from "Atsiagbeko," a narrative dance depicting past acts of bravery in war and the blessings of peace. The master drummer dictates the form of the dance: a series of drum patterns, each of which has its prescribed dance movement. He signals the switch from one pattern to another. In this short segment, try to hear the master drummer, the double metal bell pattern, and the supporting parts played on three other types of drums. The player of a rattle keeps the basic pulse.*

The player of bell and each of the supporting drummers repeats his own pattern, as notated here. Pulses are separated by bars. The patterns are both rhythmic and timbral: the sequence of high (x) and low (•) sounds is as important as the rhythm of the stroke placement.

First, invent your own set of mnemonic syllables for speaking each of the patterns. They should be different for contrasting sounds made on each drum. Speak each pattern until it is easy.

Then listen to CD track 5 and try to follow each of the instruments. Listen for only one at a time.

| | • | | | • | | | • | • | | | • | | | • | | | • | *double bell* |

| | | • | • | | • | • | | | • | • | | | • | • | *3 supporting* |

| x | x | x | • | • | • | x | x | x | • | | • | • | *drums played* |

| x | | | • | | | • | | x | | | • | x | | | • | *with sticks* |

Ruth Stone identifies this rhythmic practice as one manifestation of an aesthetic idea, a love of what she calls "faceting." Each participant contributes a facet (a segment) to the whole.

As I talked to Kpelle musicians about what kinds of performance they most valued, they told me that the highest form was when musicians combined short sound segments to create the synchronized whole. Such faceting is considered to be quite wonderful and much to be valued over everyone singing or playing in unison. When a ruler, such as a chief, appears at an official function, his presence and bearing are enhanced by what is played. A few chiefs have horn ensembles, and the audience that observes this spectacle has come to value the horns creating a composition that requires split-second timing and symbolizes the ultimate in cooperation between multiple players. So the most valued form of music is attached to the political leader who uses these sounds to reinforce his status.

Strikingly, this most performative practice for the organization of musical time reveals ways in which people make music meaningful and useful in their lives.

Music in the African Diaspora.   A number of musical genres of the African diaspora organize time at least partially through the constant unchanging articulation of a rhythm pattern that is a grouping rather than a metric structure. In Caribbean and Latin American dance genres such as *salsa*, *rumba*, *tango*, and *cha cha*, the bell pattern is transformed to **clave**. In Caribbean and Latin American music, *clave* is the term for a rhythmic pattern that is repeated constantly and without change as a rhythmic foundation for a musical selection; it organizes the rhythmic feel of the music. In her volume on the United States in this series, Reyes discusses *clave* as a musical marker of ethnic identity: "Heard by itself or as part of an ensemble, it is immediately identified as Latino, or more specifically, Afro-Caribbean."

A number of musical genres of the African diaspora—among them *salsa*—feature polyrhythmic organization of time. *Salsa*, with its three-drum percussion coordination plus other instruments, displays a thickening of the rhythmic texture beyond *clave*. Each instrument has a distinctive rhythm or rhythms (*ritmo*) to play. *Ritmo* refers to the quality of each one of them and also to the overall effect when they coordinate. The quality is defined by timing, volume, timbre, and the manner of blending with other rhythms. Perhaps most significantly, rhythmic thinking is crucial for everyone, because both melodic and percussion instruments are approached like drums. Musicians talk about playing *afincao* (i.e., locked together), meaning that if the rhythms are not happening "together," the music is "not happening." The quality of the rhythmic ensemble, which ultimately is all the ensemble, is of utmost importance (Marisol Berrios-Miranda, personal communication, 2001).

Revealing a synthesis of different musical ideas about the organization of time, Afro-Caribbean and Afro-North and South American polyrhythm is not held together by the African timeline; rather, its rhythmic groupings work within the context of meter. *Salsa* is in duple meter with measures of four counts, but it is a two-measure long *clave* pattern that really identifies it. On CD track 4, moments from a *salsa*, the *clave* can be heard played on the wooden idiophone called clave, whose timbre stands out from the drums and other instruments and voice.

With the evidence of just the systems discussed in this chapter, it is clear that the organization of time in music reveals the remarkable musical imagination of humankind. I shall now move to another element having to do with musical time—tempo, or speed.

SPEED

Musicians manipulate speed by two basic means: they focus either on the pace of the basic beat or on subdividing the basic beat.

ACTIVITY 3.14 *Compare the pace of the basic beat of your favorite dances or other types of music. What is the slowest? What is the fastest? To answer this you have to go back to that basic point: find the beat!*

Once a speed is established for the basic beat, both **acceleration** (speeding up) and **deceleration** (slowing down) might be used in the structuring of time in a musical selection. You have already learned about *rubato*—ebb and flow in the pace of the basic beat. But tradition dictates that North Indian classical instrumentalists will gradually accelerate the beat of a selection; never falling back, they sometimes attain a breathtaking speed that requires incredible virtuosity. Conversely, gradually slowing down, **ritardando**, to end a piece occurs in many styles.

In the performance of "Marieke" on CD track 33, the effect of changing the pace of the basic beat is quite dramatic. Rather than slowing at the end, the speed accelerates. "Marieke" invokes images of World War I (1914–18) in the songwriter Jacques Brel's native Belgium. As a way of bypassing French defenses and attacking Paris directly, German forces marched across the fields of Flanders, resulting in some of the bloodiest fighting of the war. Buildings, roads, nature were completely destroyed, leaving only mud and leveled land. In the churned-up soil, wild poppies began to grow. Heralded in the poem "In Flanders Fields" by the Canadian poet John McCrae, published shortly thereafter, the poppies came to symbolize the tragedy and sacrifice of the war: "In Flanders fields the poppies blow/Between the crosses, row on row." In "Marieke" the loss of a loved one (a woman) is mourned (expressed in English), as is the damage to "my fatherland" (in Flemish), with its once-flourishing cities of Bruges and Ghent (in French) (figure 3.3). As if running to escape both memories, "the day is done" comes faster and faster until the song ends in shrill hopelessness.

The second way to achieve a sense of greater speed is by increasing the subdivisions of the beat. In the performance of South Indian music, for instance, the pace of the basic beat, once established, should not change. For variety in the element of speed, therefore, musicians play with subdividing the basic beats. What changes is the rhythmic density; the speed of what fills each beat increases.

South Indian musicians speak rhythmic syllables (mnemonics, solfège) in patterns that can be used conveniently to demonstrate this

"MARIEKE"

Ay, Marieke, Marieke, the Flanders sun
shuns the sky, since you are gone.
Ay, Marieke, Marieke, in Flanders Fields
the poppies die since you are gone.

Zonder liefde, warmede liefde
wait de wind de stomme wind.
Zonder liefde, warmede liefde
weent de zee, de grijze zee.
Zonder liefde, warmede liefde
Lijdt het licht, het donker licht.
En schuurt het zand over mign land.
Mijn platte land, mijn Vlaanderen land.

Without love, warm love,
wails the wind, the speechless wind.
Without love, warm love,
Moans the sea, the grizzled sea
Without love, warm love,
Suffers the light with darkening sky
And scours the sand o'er my land
My leveled land, my Flemish land.

Ay, Marieke, Marieke, the stars look down
So soon, so soon, the day is done
Ay, Marieke, Marieke,
The Flanders moon won't light your way,
The day is done.

Zonder liefde, warmede liefde
wait de wind, (c'est fini)
Zonder liefde, warmede liefde
Weent de zee (déjà fini)
Zonder liefde, warmede liefde
Lijdt het licht (toute est fini)
En schuurt het zand over mign land
Mijn platte land, mijn Vlaanderen land.

Without love, warm love
Wails the wind (it's over)
Without love, warm love
Wails the sea (already ended)
Without love, warm love
Suffers the light (all is over)
And scours the sand o'er my land
My leveled land, my Flemish land

Ay, Marieke, Marieke, the bells have rung
the echoes sound. The day is done
Ay, Marieke, Marieke. In Flanders fields
The echoes sound, the day is done.

Zonder liefde, warmede liefde
Lacht de duivel, de zwarte duivel.
Zonder liefde, warmede liefde
Brandt mijn hart, mijn oude hart.
Zonder liefde, warmede liefde
Sterft de zomer, de droeve zomer.

Without love, warm love
Laughs the devil, the dark black devil.
Without love, warm love,
Burns up my heart, my aging heart.
Without love, warm love,
Dies the summer, the pitiful summer.

En schuurt het zand over mign land.	*And scours the sand o'er my land,*
mijn platte land, mijn Vlaanderen land.	*My leveled land, my Flemish land.*

Ay, Marieke, Marieke, come back again
come back again, the day is done.
Ay, Marieke, Marieke, Reviens le temps
Reviens le temps
Bring back the days of Bruges and Ghent
de Bruges et Gand

Ay, Marieke, Marieke, come back again
Your love alone, the day is done
Ay, Marieke, Marieke, your love alone
Come back again, the day is done
Come back again, the day is done
Come back again, the day is done

the day is done

the day is done

FIGURE 3.3 *"Marieke." words and music by Eric Blau, Jacques Brel, Gerard Jouannest.* *(Translation courtesy of Suzanne Lake)*

practice of increasing the rhythmic density within a single beat, spoken as "Ta." In the list below, items 2–4 constitute the basic subdivisions, then 5–9 use those again, in combinations. Capital T's make that clear.

1. Ta
2. Taka
3. Takita
4. Takadimi
5. TakaTakita (2 + 3)
6. TakaTakadimi (2 + 4)
7. TakitaTakadimi (3 + 4)
8. TakitaTakitaTaka (3 + 3 + 2)
9. TakaTakitaTakadimi (2 + 3 + 4)

ACTIVITY 3.15 *To experience this principle of increasing the rhythmic density, set a very slow, steady beat (•) and clap to sound it out. Then start speaking these patterns to fill in the beats, keeping the pace of the beat steady. If you feel really ambitious, carry it through the nine patterns.*

•	•	•	•
Ta	Ta	Ta	Ta
Ta ka	Ta ka	Ta ka	Ta ka
Ta ki ta	Ta ki ta	Ta ki ta	Ta ki ta
Ta ka di mi	Ta ka di mi	Ta ka di mi	Ta ka di mi
Ta kaTakita	Ta kaTakita	Ta kaTa kita	Ta kaTakita

Through subdivisions of the beat, musicians in an ensemble can play different instruments at different speeds, with all parts linked by a common basic pulse. Music played on the Central Javanese *gamelans* demonstrates this clearly. The register (see chapter 4) on each instrument correlates with the rhythmic density of its musical part: the higher the pitch, the denser the part. When you hear an extremely slow basic melody in this music, listen for extremely fast playing on some instruments (CD track 8).

In this chapter on the organization of time I have presented some ideas and practices by which musicians mark the passage of time through musical selections. Those ideas range from successions of unequal durations in freely floating rhythm, to a single regular unit—a pulse—to various kinds of meters, and to colotomic structure, rhythmic mode, and polyrhythm. Finally, I considered the element of speed, the pace of moving through time. In chapter 4 I take up the musical element of pitch.

CHAPTER 4

Thinking about Pitch

∞

I treat the subject of pitch at some length in this book for two connected reasons: pitch is the fundamental element in both melody and harmony, and ideas about pitch need to be explored in order to understand how melody and harmony are cultivated in different traditions. Accordingly, I will start by analyzing pitch in basic terms—as single **tones** and in the formation of intervals and scales. Then I will proceed to the use of pitch in melody (thinking horizontally) and in harmony (thinking vertically). This metaphorical use of "horizontal" and "vertical" comes from Western staff notation, where melodies are notated from left to right and harmonies are aligned vertically.

In its most generic sense, **melody** can be defined as any selection of pitches in succession. A particular melody will have one of several forms. It might be short—as in a **motive** (CD track 40). It might be relatively longer, as in an Irish tune (CD track 37) or a mariachi strophe (CD track 29), or even longer, as in a jazz riff of several sections or the solos of a Japanese *syakuhati* (vertical bamboo flute) player (figure 2.8, CD track 15). A melody can be easy to sing or play for those familiar with the melodic system, or difficult to remember.

In its most generic sense, **harmony** can be defined as pitches heard simultaneously. How the relationship between those pitches is understood differs from system to system.

PITCH

∞

"Ken McIntyre once commented that a great improviser could play an entire solo based on one pitch alone. Coincidentally, during an interview with a young drummer, a soft background recording featured flugelhornist Wilbur Hardin, who was gen-

*erating tremendous excitement with a stream of single-pitched
rhythmic patterns at his solo's opening. . . . The drummer
suddenly burst out laughing and, with an apology for his dis-
traction, added: 'Did you hear that? That's what our music's about. Listen to all that brother can say with one note!'"
(Berliner, 1994: 147).*

∞

The term **pitch** as a relative quality of "highness" or "lowness" of
sound is not limited to musical terminology: we speak of the high-
pitched squeal of tires and the low-pitched roar of a powerful motorcycle engine. Musical pitch is a more focused idea, referring to a sound
that is produced more purposefully in some area, high to low.

In terms of musical practice around the world, it is useful to think
of a continuum of ideas about pitch placement. At one end is a sense
of satisfaction when the pitch lies anywhere within an expected general
compass. In his case study of East African music in this series, Greg
Barz cites the distinguished Ugandan musician Centurio Balikoowa as
saying: "The temperature in our country is sometimes a bit hot, and the
instruments, apart from the flutes, they respond to the weather. If it's
hot they go very high. If it's cool it goes very low. So people just play
without thinking that this is [this pitch] or this is [that pitch as on a key-
board]." At the other end of the continuum is the ideal of precise placement, a pitch that results when a string, a column of air, or other sound-
producing body vibrates at a particular **frequency** (rate) such as 440
cycles per second. I will return to this concept later.

Pitch Names.   For communication about music and as an aid to memory (mnemonic), it is convenient to assign names to pitches. This has
been done in various places around the world, using syllables, numbers, or letters. A few examples are given here.

Syllables.   Syllables used to name pitches (and percussion strokes) are
generically called by the term **solfège**. In India historically syllables have
been assigned to seven pitches in ascending order as *sa, re* (in North India, *ri* in South India), *ga, ma, pa, dha* (in North India, *da* in South India), and *ni*. On CD track 30, those syllables are incorporated into vocal music as text for melody; this brief excerpt sung by the late great
Pandit Amir Khan begins *"re—ni sa."* Indian musicians notate music by
writing those syllables, and they appear prominently in the case studies on North and South India in this series.

Solfège syllables have been used in European music since about 1600, as follows: *do, re, mi, fa, sol, la,* and *ti* (or *si*), in ascending order. The song "Doe, a deer, a female deer," from the Broadway musical *The Sound of Music,* plays with those syllables, as in "Ray, a drop of golden sun;/Me, a name I call myself." That song occurs as the nanny is giving the children a singing lesson. In fact, that system of solfège is used for teaching music around the world; it has been widely adopted throughout the Middle East, and musicians in Arab countries, Turkey, and Iran are masters at singing and sight-reading in solfège.

Numbers.   Numbers are used in music in at least two different ways. One is to indicate pitch (*do* = 1, *re* = 2, etc.). The other use is technical, instructing musicians how to produce a particular pitch on an instrument. This is the case with the tablature for the Chinese *qin* (figure 1.7, 1.9), (where notation tells the player which string to pluck). In Javanese music, where basic melodies are played out on metal xylophone-type instruments, the slabs are numbered (figure 1.5). On the *qin* and the metallophone, the resulting melodies depend on which pitches the strings or slabs are tuned to.

Letters.   In the European system, letters as well as syllables and numbers are used for identifying pitches. Adopted from Arabic in the early Middle Ages, the letters in ascent are A, B, C, D, E, F, and G. Interestingly, the present-day Arab world does not use this letter system, preferring either European solfège or traditional Arab or Persian names for the notes.

Setting the Pitch.   Questions arise. Where is pitch *sa* or pitch 1 or pitch A? Who sets the pitch, and how?

Who Sets the Pitch.   On many instruments the pitch is fixed in construction. During manufacture, a flute will have pitch holes drilled at some points; on a metallophone, the metal will be forged and then trimmed to produce a certain pitch when struck. On the metal surface of a steel drum discretely tuned spots will be hammered out (figure 4.1). **Frets** (perpendicular bars or strings running under several strings) can be supplied on the instrument to indicate the place of other desired pitches. Most but not all fretted stringed instruments are lutes (figure 4.2); the zither-type Korean *komungo* has frets (figure 2.9; CD track 17). If they are to be fixed in place, the instrument maker will have to know the musical system in order to set the pitches properly.

FIGURE 4.1   *Steel drum with pitches labeled.*   *(Photo by Phuoc Truong)*

If the pitches are not fixed on the instrument, the musician has responsibility for setting them. On the Japanese *koto* (figure 2.8), the player positions a moveable **bridge** under each string to set its pitch, and a player of a lute-type instrument such as the *syamisen* in figure 2.8 tightens the strings to a certain basic pitch. Beyond that, fretless bowed and plucked lutes present great challenges for players. To obtain pitches beyond those on their open strings, all the musicians in figure 2.2 and the *syamisen* player in figure 2.8 (CD track 41) have to memorize where to press their fingers down on the strings along the neck. They must literally embody the sense of pitch as they train their muscles what to do.

ACTIVITY 4.1   *If you know how to tune an instrument, articulate that process to someone who is unfamiliar with it. In addition, get someone to explain the process on an instrument you are less familiar with.*

FIGURE 4.2 *Salsa Band. Left front, Héctor Pérez (bongos); right center, Rafael Angel Irizarry (Puerto Rican cuatro); right front, Jorgé Martínez (guitarrón); right rear, Marisol Berrios-Miranda (güiro); rear left, Karim A. Imes (drum set); rear right, Allan Stone (bass). The bongo drums (front left) are tuned the interval of a fourth apart. Note the bridges on the sounding board of each of the plucked lutes, and the frets up the necks, as well as the tuning pegs on the guitar on the left rear. (Photo by Kathleen Karn)*

Pitch Placement. At what sound levels pitches should lie is a matter of choice in a musical style, deeply embedded in tradition.

All musicians have an ideal of pitch precision, but the ideals differ widely. Indonesian traditions provide a good example of this. In Central Java, each ensemble (*gamelan*) of instruments is manufactured to have its own distinctive set of pitches (figure 1.5). No two ensembles are tuned alike, and the aesthetic effect of its tuning gives each *gamelan* a musical identity.

In Bali, precise tuning is done with pairs of instruments. However, the two instruments in a pair are tuned precisely *unalike*: the frequencies (the rate of vibration of the sound waves) of their pitches are very close but intentionally set far enough apart in order to produce **beats**. Beats occur when two sound waves with different frequencies overlap; what we hear are resulting periodic variations in loudness. This is demonstrated on CD track 42, with each instrument played alone, then the two instruments together. The practice of paired tunings creates the desired bright, shimmering metallic timbre that you hear in CD track 31. The contrasting pitch ideals in the Central Javanese *gamelan* on CD track 8 and the Balinese *gamelan* on CD track 31 make the ensemble sounds unmistakably different.

In classical music in the European system the named pitches (A, B, C, D, etc.) are expected to lie at some precise place, that is, at a precise frequency: by agreement in recent times, the pitch called "A above middle C" vibrates at 440 cycles per second (with some preference also for the slightly higher pitch of 442 cps). Instruments with fixed pitch are manufactured to this standard, and instrumentalists without fixed pitch are expected to adjust to it. This adjustment can be witnessed and heard through the tuning practice that initiates an orchestra concert (CD track 43). Before the conductor of the orchestra comes onstage and the performance begins in a formal sense, the **concert master** or **concert mistress** (leader of the violin section, who acts as an assistant to the conductor) stands to face the orchestra and instructs the lead player of the oboe section to produce the pitch A. In turn, in a ritualized order the sections of the orchestra tune. From the cacophony that soon results, it is clear that this is also an opportunity to warm up onstage. Furthermore, the tuning cues the audience to settle into silence for the performance, a practice derived from and idiosyncratic of European classical music performance.

With a sense of "in-tuneness" firmly established in one's musical soundscape, playing against it can be an aesthetic choice. One need only think of the "bent notes" that play around with pitches' "in-tuneness"; modern keyboard synthesizers have wheels on them so the keyboardist can bend the notes. The *salsa* musician Gerardo Rosales insists that *salsa* is not authentic *salsa* unless the trombonist plays a little bit out of tune; not all *salsa* musicians agree, however (Berrios-Miranda 1999).

For a performer to produce pitches at the desired frequencies is known as "having good **intonation**." An ideal once held by musicians of European classical music was to "have **perfect pitch**," wherein one could identify or produce a desired letter-named musical pitch at its established frequency even if asked on the spot; now it is considered far more useful to "have excellent relative pitch." That is certainly the case if you want to enjoy music of traditions with different senses of intonation. A sensible, flexible way to think about "good intonation" is to appreciate musicians' exceptional ability to remember what they hear, in whatever pitch system they cultivate.

A finely cultivated sense of pitch is crucial also in the classical music of North India. Producing pitches that are out of tune with the expected pitch placement is sufficient in contemporary times to ruin a musician's reputation, but it has always been so; from the *Nāradīya Śikṣā* (c. fourth century C.E.): "Wrong musical intonation is a crime in which one risks one's life, one's progeny, and one's cattle" (te Nijenhuis 1974: 36). Flexibility is embedded within the system, however: there is no standardized pitch frequency (cycles per second) for the pitch called *sa*. *Sa* can be placed anywhere a singer is comfortable placing it—not so high or so low as to prevent reaching all the pitches desired in the improvisatory moments to come.

ACTIVITY 4.2 *Experiment with singing a straight ascending row of pitches, calling them* sa re ga ma pa dha ni sa re ga ma. *Start the* sa *on several different pitch levels and listen and feel the difference. Finally, find "your* sa," *a place to start where it is most comfortable to sing up that number of pitches.*

All of the preceding discussion about pitch assumes that a pitch is a discrete entity, a sound. To musicians in some traditions there is much more to it. In Korean musical aesthetics, for instance, the moments of the sounding are just part of the aural experiencing of a pitch. Its dying away, its decay as a string gradually ceases to vibrate audibly, is at the heart of the aesthetic sense, as well: the beauty of "sound into silence."

THINKING HORIZONTALLY

Intervals. In the discussion above I focused primarily on single pitches, but here I want to move to thinking about pitches in relationship to each other. That relationship can be horizontal—that is, a succession of pitches, as in melody—or vertical—that is, in some kind of harmonic simultaneity. In either case, it is the distance spanned between pitches that comes into play. The English-language term for that distance is **interval**. The matter of intervals is more important in music in

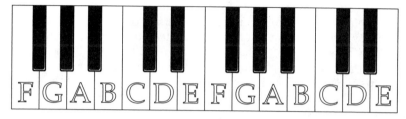

FIGURE 4.3   *Keyboard with white keys named.*   *(Chart by Viet Nyugen)*

the European system than in any other, because that system cultivates harmonic relationships. Nevertheless, I shall approach intervals first as pitches occurring one after another (horizontally), as in melody.

Naming Intervals.   So important are intervals in European music theory that they are given names. Two factors are involved in the naming. One is the number of pitches that the interval spans. Figure 4.3 depicts a keyboard with the white keys labeled A, B, C, D, E, F, and G.

Ascending from A to B involves two pitch letters; the interval from A to B is thus called a second. Going up from A to C spans across A, B, and C (i.e., three pitch letters), so the interval is called a third, and so forth. The interval from one note to another note with the same letter name spans eight pitch letters and is called an **octave** (*octo-*, "eight"), as in A to the next higher (or lower) A.

ACTIVITY 4.3   *Practice singing and naming intervals in both ascending and descending order: second, third, fourth, fifth, sixth, seventh, octave. Say the letter name of the pitch as you sing it. For example: to sing an ascending fourth from A, sing A, B, C, D, then sing the two outside pitches back and forth—A and D, D and A—to get the feel of it.*

The second factor involved in the naming of intervals in the European system is the type or quality of the interval. There are different types of seconds, thirds, fourths, and the like. Looking again at the keyboard (figure 4.3), you can see two types of seconds. Between pitches

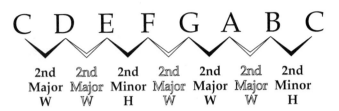

FIGURE 4.4   *Two ways of naming the interval of a second.*   *(Chart by Viet Nguyen)*

B and C (the interval of a second) and E and F (also a second), there is no intervening key. Between F and G (also a second), however, there is an intervening key. The size of the second between F and G is wider: it is called a **major second**. The interval between E and F is the smaller second, called a **minor second**.

Seconds are named in another way as well: the major second is called a **whole step** (in figure 4.4 labeled *W*). The minor second is a **half step** (in Figure 4.4 labeled *H*). Figure 4.5 shows how, on the piano keyboard, the interval between any two adjacent keys is a half step.

Just as there are two types of seconds, there are two sizes of thirds—major and minor thirds. To explore these, see Activity 4.4.

ACTIVITY 4.4   *On the keyboard, count the number of half steps in the third from C to E. You should find four. This is a major third. Or think of it this way: two whole steps make a major third.*

FIGURE 4.5   *Half steps on the piano keyboard.*   *(Chart by Viet Nguyen)*

> *Now count the number of half steps in the third from E to G. There are only three half steps (or, a whole step and a half step). This is a minor third.*
>
> *Major and minor thirds are crucial intervals for you to hear and feel. One way to do it is to sing the familiar melody of "Frère Jacques" (CD track 44): the melody on just those two first words of the song outline a major third, first in ascent and then in descent. You might know this as "Are you sleeping?"; in that case, the major third occurs on "Are . . . sleeping." Sing it several times. Once you have that interval in your ears, try to lower the pitch on "Jac/sleep" by a half step; the melody will sound very different with a minor third.*

Microtones.   Many musical systems use intervals smaller than the half step, the smallest named interval in Western music; such intervals are sometimes called **microtones**. Another term, **quarter tone** is frequently used to describe an interval that evenly divides the half step. Combined with larger intervals, quarter tones create intervals that fall exactly between the Western major and minor seconds, or between the major and minor thirds. In Arab music, these are referred to as "half-flat" intervals—half-flat seconds or half-flat thirds, for example. *Maqam Rast*, a melodic mode explored in depth in Scott Marcus's volume on music of the Middle East in this series, features a half-flat third and a half-flat seventh (CD track 25).

> **ACTIVITY 4.5**   *Listen to the beginning of CD track 25, the instrumental introduction to a song by the great Egyptian singer Umm Kulthum. In the melodic unit (phrase) that immediately follows the downbeat given by the double bass, the second note is a half-flat third. The penultimate note of that phrase is a half-flat seventh. The phrase repeats. Listen to the opening section several times, up to the beginning of the* qanun *(plucked frame zither) solo.*

Scale. Theorists and practitioners in a number of musical systems think about melodic material in terms of pitch sets—groups of pitches. One clear way to articulate a set of pitches is to present them as a scale, in straight ascending or descending order. (Note: this is not appropriate for some types of pitch sets.) When one hears a scale, the focus can be on the pitches or on the intervals formed by the distances between the pitches. In Indian music theory, for instance, the focus is on the pitches, while in the European system the focus is on the intervals. I shall sample a few scale types and illustrate how scalar material might be used in melodic practice.

The Chromatic Scale.   Sounding all twelve pitches in an octave on the piano in ascending or descending order produces what in English is called a **chromatic scale**.

ACTIVITY 4.6   *Find a keyboard and use figure 4.5 to position a finger on pitch C, in about the middle of the keyboard. Play each key in succession (both white and black) up to the next pitch C. You have created a chromatic scale of twelve pitches.*

A dramatic example of the chromatic scale in melody is the opening of the famous aria "L'amour est un oiseau rebelle," from *Carmen*, an opera by the French composer Georges Bizet (1838–75). Much of the first part of the aria consists of a descending chromatic scale. (This aria is more commonly called "Habanera," which is actually the Cuban song form that supposedly served as the stylistic basis for the aria.)

ACTIVITY 4.7   *At the point in the story of the opera* Carmen *that is recorded on CD track 21, a number of female factory workers mill about onstage, trying to attract the attention of soldiers who wait instead for the sensually flirtatious heroine, Carmen. The excerpt begins as she finally enters. Carmen is interested only in a soldier whom she does not see.*

First listen to CD track 21 all the way through, for the purpose of following the French text (even if you do not know French).

The quick orchestral introduction to the aria begins at 1:02. Be ready to listen for the chromatic scale at the beginning of the aria. Occurrences of chromatic melody are underlined in the French text. You will hear it better if you try to sing along with the soloist. Keep listening, because that melody repeats.

(Carmen enters)

0: 05 All

La voilà!

There she is!

0:17 Men

Carmen, sur tes pas,
  nous nous pressons tous;

Carmen, we're all at your feet!

Carmen, sois gentille, au
  moins réponds-nous,

Carmen, be kind and at least
  answer us,

Et dis-nous quel jour tu
  nous aimeras.

and say that one day you'll love us!

Carmen, dis-nous quel jour
  tu nous aimeras.

Carmen, say which day you will
  love us!

0:33 Carmen

Quand je vous aimerai?
Ma foi, je ne sais pas.

(after a quick glance at Don José)
When will I love you?
Really, I don't know.

Peut-être jamais,
  peut-être demain,
Mais pas aujourd'hui,
  c'est certain.

Perhaps never, perhaps tomorrow,

  but not today—that's certain.

1:08

L'amour est un oiseau rebelle
que nul ne peut apprivoiser.
Et c'est bien en vain
  qu'on l'appelle,
S'il lui convient de refuser.
Rien n'y fait; menace ou prière.
L'un parles bien, l'autre se tait;

Habanera
Love is a bird wild and free
  whom no one can tame;
And it's useless to appeal to him,

  if he's in the mood to refuse.
He heeds no threat or prayer.
One speaks well, the other is silent;

Et c'est l'autre que je préfère.
Il n'a rien dit, mais il me plait.
 pleases me.

and it's the other whom I prefer.
He has said nothing; but he

1:36 Chorus
L'amour est un oiseau rebelle
que nul ne peut apprivoiser.
Et c'est bien en vain qu'on
 l'appelle,
S'il lui convient de refuser.

Love is a bird wild and free
whom no one can tame;
and it's useless to appeal
 to him,
if he's in the mood to refuse.

1:37 Carmen
Amour, amour, amour, amour!
L'amour est enfant de Bohême,
Il n'a jamais, jamais
connu de loi.
Si tu ne m'aimes pas, je t'aime.
Et si je t'aime,
prend garde à toi!

(first line overlapping with chorus)
Love, love, love, love!
Love is a gypsy child
who never, never heeds
any law.
If you don't love me, I love you;
And if I love you—
ah then, beware!

2:05 Chorus
Prends garde à toi!

Ah then, beware!

Continue to listen for repetition of the last three lines and the verse from
 the beginning of the "Habanera."

Long chromatic descents and ascents and quick three-pitch chromatic
motives comprise much of the melodic material in the contemporary
piece "Mini Overture" by the Polish composer Witold Lutosławski
(1913–94) (CD track 28). This is a snappy fanfare for brass quintet.
Within seconds of the start, the first trumpeter gives out a descending
chromatic alarum, which is taken up in turn by the horn and trombone
players. Immediately after, the trombonist initiates the idea of repeating three-pitch chromatic motives, answered very quickly by the second trumpeter and then the horn player. From that point you can hear
rapid three-pitch chromatic motives that seem to be everywhere: 1:02
to 1:35 is thick with them, also at 1:55. The long chromatic line recurs
at 2:35, recalling the beginning at the end.

Diatonic Scales. **Diatonic scales** comprise some arrangement of half
steps and whole steps. If you have grown up hearing music in the Eu-

ropean system, and you just sing the most natural scale that comes into your head, you will no doubt sing one of them—the **major scale**. You have learned it by osmosis. It is the scale you sing on the text syllables "Doe, ray, me, far, sew, la, and tea" in "Doe, a deer" (that is, the solfège syllables *do, re, mi, fa, sol, la,* and *ti* or *si*). Figure 4.4 shows a major scale that begins on pitch C. You can see there the arrangement of whole steps and half steps within an octave: W W H W W W H (CD track 45).

> **ACTIVITY 4.8** *Other CD tracks you have listened to thus far have melodies that use a Western major scale. Listen again to identify at least two of them.*

Another important diatonic scale in the Western system is the **natural minor scale**. Its arrangement of whole steps and half steps is W H W W H W W. Major and minor thirds play the most significant part in distinguishing the major and minor scales.

The "Oriental" Scale. Perhaps you will immediately recognize CD track 46 as a Spanish flamenco song—by the vocal style perhaps, or by the guitar style. The scale in the melody might also sound familiar to you; starting on C, its pitches are C D^b E F G Ab B. You have not yet encountered in this book the interval between pitches 2 and 3, and between pitches 6 and 7; because it spans two letter names, it must be a second of some kind, yet it encompasses three half steps. Larger than a major second, this **augmented second** distinguishes this scale from a diatonic scale and establishes its "difference." The music of the excerpt on CD track 46 is so particular to flamenco that the scale is strongly associated with the Roma, who developed the style. Non-Romani composers have used this and similar nondiatonic scales to suggest not only the Roma but also other exotic people and places in "orientalist" fashion (Said 1978). For that reason, this scale is sometimes called the "**Oriental scale**." Because the word "oriental" now connotes derogatory colonialist attitudes, English speakers today use the term with caution. But the connotations of the musical scale continue unabated, and the use of it may outlast use of the word "oriental."

Number of Pitches in an Octave. To consider scales on a worldwide basis, it is useful to think in terms of the number of pitches that lie within an octave. There are numerous **heptatonic** (seven-tone) scales, of which the European major scale is one (CD track 45). **Pentatonic** (five-tone) scales are also numerous, such as the scale of "Auld Lang Syne" (C, D, E, G, A), sung to mark the beginning of a new year.

ACTIVITY 4.9 *To experience music with two different pentatonic pitch selections, first sing "Auld Lang Syne." Then listen to CD track 8, a selection in a Javanese tuning system called* slendro, *which is pentatonic. While the pentatonic scale of "Auld Lang Syne" has a clear "gap" between pitches E and G, Javanese* slendro *positions the five pitches more or less equidistantly within an octave.*

Pitch Functions.   Whether you have a set of five, six, twelve or some other number of pitches in a set, the idea of assigning some particular function to one or more of them is widespread. A South Indian classical *rāga* (**melodic mode**) is likely to have a beginning pitch, an ending pitch, and "life-giving tone(s)" on which the melody pauses and dwells.

An extremely common musical practice is to establish a **pitch hierarchy**; that is to say, some pitch in a pitch set is given more importance in melody than other pitches. Ethnomusicologists have called it various things: a **tonal center**, a base note, a fundamental, or a primary pitch. One can often sense a tonal center in listening to melody, perhaps because the pitch occurs frequently or because the melody comes to an end on it. The best way to locate a tonal center is simply to listen and let it emerge in your hearing—and not worry if you cannot sense it at first.

ACTIVITY 4.10 *Try feeling the tonal center in these selections: CD track 2, "Gunslingers" (steelband); CD track 3, "Partridges Flying" (Chinese ensemble); CD track 7, "Ballad of César Chávez"; and CD track 44, "Frère Jacques" ("Are you sleeping").*

In the European tradition the tonal center is called a **tonic**, and the system of music that is organized around having a functional tonic is called **tonal music**. It is appropriate to think of "tonic" as a "home pitch" because in tonal music aesthetics there is a definite sense of finality associated with returning to the tonic pitch to end a piece. You can feel this clearly on CD track 32, "West End Blues."

Any pitch in the European system can be the tonic of a major or minor scale. The resulting tonality is identified as a **key**: the key of A major (A is *do*) or the key of A minor; the key of D major (D is *do*) or the key of D minor. Keys are useful in several ways, one of which is performing music at a pitch register that is comfortable for your voice or on your instrument.

> **ACTIVITY 4.11** *Find a comfortable pitch for yourself, from which you can sing a major scale up, covering about an octave. Identify your comfortable key by finding the starting pitch (the tonic) on the piano.*

Hierarchy is so important in tonal music that three other pitches in a key are designated as more important functionally. The important pitch that is five pitches up from the tonic is called the **dominant**; in "Take Five" (CD track 24) the bass player articulates the metric structure by alternating between the tonic and dominant. The pitch located four pitches up from the tonic is the **subdominant**. A third important pitch is generally called the **leading tone**; located a half step below the tonic (or, in the less common case of the "upper leading tone," a half step above tonic), it is used to create a feeling of going toward the tonic.

Mode. Beyond the rather abstract idea of pitches and their functions, intervals, and scales is another entirely different way of thinking about what constitutes fundamental melodic material on which compositions and improvisation are based. That is **mode**, an idea about pitch and melody that encompasses both explicitly musical practice and extra-musical associations. Rajna Klaser has described the way she learned about mode in Turkish music, there termed **makam**.

> Every Tuesday morning I would meet my teacher, Yusuf Ömürlü Bey, for my lesson. Each time, he would have ready two identical binders containing select vocal and instrumental pieces in one *makam*. With

these binders on his desk—one for him, the other for me—introduction of a new *makam* would commence. As he is browsing through the sheets deciding which tune we will start our lesson with, Yusuf Ömürlu Bey is humming in free rhythm a vocal improvisation, a *seyir* of a *makam* I am about to learn. This little ritual is followed by his explanation of the properties of the *makam*. He would write a scalar formation of a *makam*, clearly defining its tonic and dominant with whole notes, delineating its tetrachord and pentachord with arches, showing acoustical relationships between adjacent notes with standard symbols [letters] and also the general melodic progression of the *makam*.

FIGURE 4.6 *Turkish* makam *Hicaz*.

Up to this point, Yusuf Ömürlu Bey's instruction is very systematic and does not depart from the explanations one can find in textbooks on Turkish music theory. His instruction is musically mute, my teacher never finding any reason to demonstrate either the scale or those nuances with his voice.

From that point, however, Yusuf Ömürlu Bey's instruction departs to the more illusive and poetic realm of "colors" [*renkler*] or "fragrances" [*kokular*] of the *makam* in question. This is where his passion for Turkish music and Turkish melody becomes obvious. As he demonstrates with his voice these *colors and fragrances in the form of characteristic motif, change in register, shift to important functional degrees, and melodic alterations that give particular identity* to the *makam*, his facial expressions depict *the emotional feel* of the *makam* that puts it into the realm of poetry. He frequently describes them with poetical tropes such as melancholy, happiness, and so forth. As a conclusion, Yusuf Ömürlu Bey hums another vocal improvisation demonstrating discussed features of the *makam* for that day, and segues into singing several vocal and instrumental compositions from the binder. (Klaser 2001: 62–4)

In the quote, I have italicized those characteristics—particular expressive qualities—that make mode a more encompassing idea about melodic material than even the composite of pitch and pitch function, interval, scale, and key.

The words "mode" and "mood" are linguistically related and musically articulated. "If you take any set of notes and continually play only these notes, then a mood is built up. After a long period of hearing only these notes, adding a new note creates a shock. Similarly, by playing only a different set of notes, a different mode is created" (Scott Marcus, personal communication, 2001).

Musicians in North India consider their melodic modes (*rāga*) bearers of special expressive capacity to communicate moods. Some historians explain that capacity by citing the ancient connection of music and drama, where the shifting moods in a play would be expressed musically. Other historians connect it with the shifting natural moods in a day, from meditative in the early morning hours, to energetic in mid-morning, tantalizingly tentative at sunrise and sunset, and serious in the late night. Others explain it through the different contexts and functions of music in a complex court culture in which India's classical music was cultivated—music for religious worship, light after-dinner entertainment, serious discussion deep in the night. Perhaps it is a combination of nature and culture. Whatever the reason, meditative *Rāga Āsāvarī*, with all its particular modal characteristics, is best performed in early morning. The Malhar *rāga*s are best performed in the monsoon season, when, perhaps, they might relieve the oppressively humid atmosphere by causing a cloudburst (or by bringing a beloved, who is as awaited as the rain).

Melodic mode with all its characteristics and associations is fully explored in the Middle East and India volumes in this series.

THINKING VERTICALLY

In the discussion above, I focused on pitch as the fundamental material for melody. Here I shift to thinking about pitches that are heard simultaneously (vertically), bringing harmonic orientation into play. The amount of focus on vertical relationships and the nature of them differs from music to music; no musical system cultivates verticality as much as does the European music system. In the discussion below, I present a few examples of ways in which musicians practice music with a vertical orientation.

Tone Clusters.   Complex tone clusters occur in Japanese *gagaku* music, played on an aerophone called the *shō*. (It is the first instrument heard on CD track 26, and the players of *shō* sit at the rear right in figure 2.14.) A **tone cluster** is a vertical set of pitches, without the functional implications of chords in the tonal system (see below). In the *shō* part in this musical tradition, the bottom pitch of the cluster and the occasional single pitch correspond to melodic pitches. The effect of the *shō* cluster is that of a complex chord played on an organ, sustained for several counts, and gradually changed to another cluster. The *shō*'s part is important to the sound of the ensemble; without it the texture becomes sparse, as you can hear in CD track 26 when its part ceases.

Naming Vertical Intervals. The term **interval** in harmonic thinking has the same meaning as in melodic thinking: the distance between two pitches. Several intervals may be heard on CD track 47; their names in European music theory are as follows: minor and major second, minor and major third, perfect fourth, augmented fourth/diminished fifth and perfect fifth, minor and major sixth, minor and major seventh, and octave. Intervals that exceed the octave are called ninth (i.e., an octave plus a second), tenth, eleventh, and so forth.

Dissonance and Consonance. The quality of the sound produced by a vertical interval is spoken of as **dissonant** or **consonant**. A widely held idea in European music theory has been that those intervals which are mathetically simple regarding the ratios of their frequencies (an octave is a simple 2:1 ratio) are "consonant." The consonant intervals are the first five of the natural overtone series: the octave, the fifth (3:2), the fourth (4:3), the major third (5:4), and the minor third (6:5). Complex intervals, on the other hand (a major second is 9:8) are "dissonant." According to this theory, dissonance produces tension, whereas consonance offers relaxation, by release of tension.

ACTIVITY 4.12 *When a pitch is produced, we hear it as a single entity, but in actuality it is a composite of the fundamental frequency plus a set of mathematically related overtones—the* **overtone series***.*

Find a stringed instrument with which to experiment. (The strings inside a piano will do, or guitar or violin strings.) To obtain the first natural overtone of the pitch to which one string is set, sound the string while lightly touching it right in the middle of its length, producing a simple 2:1 ratio; do not press so hard that you touch the sounding board. Doing so should result in a ringing pitch an octave higher than the string's pitch when played normally. To get the second overtone, experiment with finding a spot where the string is divided into three equal parts. When you find it, the pitch a fifth higher than the first overtone (i.e., an octave and a fifth higher than the string's normal pitch) will result. To get the third overtone (a fourth higher than the second overtone and two octaves higher than the starting pitch), find the spot one-fourth the length of the string.

Venturing beyond that mathematical concept of consonance and dissonance takes us into the subjective realm of musical aesthetics. For example, we find entirely different aesthetic ideas about the interval of a second: to Bulgarian women in the area of Sofia, the second is "pleasant and smooth"—in effect, consonant. In an example presented in Timothy Rice's volume on Bulgaria in this series, one woman sings the melody; another sings a part that zigzags between the tonic pitch and the note below it. They are striving to make their vertical intervals "ring like a bell" by narrowing them, especially on long-held notes, to somewhere between a major second and a minor second until they get the desired effect, an intense "beating" that is reminiscent of that produced on the paired Balinese instruments (CD track 42). The tension of singing is released at the end of a verse with a cry on the syllable "eee," leaping melodically up a seventh or an octave, and sliding down.

Nor is the idea about dissonant seconds and sevenths maintained in a good deal of contemporary composition, whether written in the tonal system or not. Lutosławski's "Mini Overture" abounds with minor seconds; they contribute part of the energy of the piece (CD track 28).

Functional Harmony.   Intervals stacked vertically in tonal music are usually understood to form **chords**. A certain chord built on pitch 1 (*do*) of a key is the tonic chord (written in Roman numerals, I); likewise, a certain chord built on pitch 5 is the dominant chord (V), a certain chord built on pitch 4 is the subdominant chord (IV), and so forth. Not surprisingly, those chords constitute a hierarchy analogous to the pitch hierarchy discussed above: the tonic chord is all-important; the dominant chord and subdominant chords are important, in that order. This use of chords is called **functional harmony**.

Chords in the tonal system consist of three or more pitches. The most basic is a **triad**, so called because it consists of three pitches, the upper two of which are stacked a third and a fifth, respectively, above the bottom pitch or root of the chord.

ACTIVITY 4.13 *To do this activity you need to gather at least two friends. Together count as you sing up from pitch 1 to 5 (starting anywhere that is comfortable for all of you), then sing just 1, 3, and 5 (leaving out 2 and 4). Sing 1–3–5–3–1 (ascent and descent) until it feels easy; those are the pitches of a triad. Then split up the pitches among you so that someone is singing each of the three pitches. When you sing them simultaneously, you are producing a triad. Build more triads, stacking thirds above any pitch.*

A sequence of chords is called a **chord progression**. In much tonal music a common practice guides which chord is likely to follow a given chord. The subdominant chord (IV) is likely to be followed by the dominant chord (V) or the tonic chord (I), for instance, and the dominant chord (V) is likely to lead to the tonic chord (I). Chord progressions of countless songs use just two or three of those chords.

ACTIVITY 4.14 *With the recording on CD track 48, sing this progression of these pitches:*
1 4 5 1 4 1 5 1 4 5 1
If you were to build chords on each one of those pitches, your chord progression would be I IV V I IV I V I IV V I. The pitches are called the root pitches of the chords.

The *corrido* "Ballad of César Chávez" (CD track 7) uses the tonic and dominant chords in a clear fashion. The guitar player anticipates the change with finger picking. Here I have rewritten the first two verses, with the chords indicated.

(Guitar intro settles on I.)

En un día siete de marzo, Jueves Santo en la mañana,

    I   V   V   I

Salió César de Delano, Componiendo una compaña.

    I   V   V   I

(Brief guitar interlude stays on I.)

Companeros campesinos   Este va a ser un ejemplo

   I   V   V   I

Esta marcha la llevamos   Hasta mero Sacramento.

   I   V   V   I

A genre of music that uses the I, IV, and V chords to the fullest is the blues. In most blues pieces, a chord progression that repeats in every verse provides stable underpinning for the flexible parts that swirl around it. Stripped to its simplest form, that chord progression is as follows.

I I I I

IV IV I I

V V I I

ACTIVITY 4.15 *Listen to the corrido on CD track 7 and try to sing the tonic and dominant pitches that undergird the chord progression.*

If you succeed at that, proceed to CD track 32, "West End Blues," a 1928 Louis Armstrong hit. Try to follow the blues chord progression when the theme begins, just after Armstrong's famous introductory trumpet solo.

The first task is to feel the tonic. Listen through the selection until you are sure you have that. Then focus on chord changes. You should expect to get all the way through the blues chord progression in the length of one chorus.

0:15 Listen to the chords in the piano through the first chorus.
0:50 The second chorus features a solo by trombonist Fred Robinson.
1:24 Armstrong sings scat syllables through the third chorus, alternating with Jimmy Strong on clarinet.
1:59 The fourth chorus features a piano solo by Earl "Fatha" Hines.
2:33 The final chorus starts with a long-held high pitch on the trumpet before Armstrong takes off again.
The piece ends on a clear, comfortable tonic chord.

THINKING HORIZONTALLY AND VERTICALLY

Now I want to consider the interplay among musical parts when groups of people make music together. The variety of melodic and harmonic practices can be heard as lying along a continuum, at one end of which is music with no vertical dimension and at the other is music in which the vertical dimension is paramount. Musical relationships among the various parts result in what many music analysts call **texture**. For a good deal of music in the European system, it is possible to classify pieces according to categories of texture, and I refer to those categories below. Many pieces, however, are not easily categorized, and when one considers other musics outside of Europe, the number of possibilities for ensemble relationships burgeons, causing many ethnomusicologists to avoid analyzing music in terms of texture altogether. In this section I shall explore some of those many possibilities, starting with ways a group of musicians might perform one melody.

Performing One Melody.
Solo and in Unison. A musical texture consisting of a single melodic line and nothing else is **monophony**, literally "one voice." Melody is monophonic if sung or played by a single person alone (**solo**), as on CD track 1, Islamic Koranic recitation, and on CD track 15, a *syakuhati* solo. It is still monophonic if that single melodic line is sung by a group of people in **unison**, either on the same pitch or in octaves. (Note: singing pitches an octave apart is musically thought of as singing "the same" pitch.) The Navajo song (CD track 9) is started as a solo, then the individual is joined by others in unison. For the first thirty-four seconds of CD track 49, the fourteenth-century song "Sumer is icumen in"

Sumer is icumen in.
Lhude sing cucu,
Groweth sed and bloweth med,
and springth the wude nu.
Sing cucu.
Awe bletheth after lomb,
Louth after calve cu;
Bulloc sterteth, bucke verteth
Murie sing cucu.
Cucu, cucu.
Wel singes thu cucu,
Ne swik thu naver nu.

FIGURE 4.7.   *"Sumer is icumen in."*

("Summer is a-coming in") is presented in unison by a mixed chorus. (The Middle English text is provided in figure 4.7). Various signs of summer are noted—seeds growing, female animals with young, and the male animals restless—but the recurring reference is to the cuckoo, whose call is imitated melodically.

Interlocking Parts.   Another way of performing a melody communally is to split it up among several musicians, assigning a single pitch or a few pitches only to each person. The melody is the sum of the parts. (This performance style was known as **hocket** in music of the late medieval period of Western history.) If you listen closely to the Peruvian panpipe selection (CD track 22), you can hear that two players combine pitches to make the melody in each part. This performance practice of **interlocking parts** occurs frequently in Balinese music also; on CD track 50 players of a group of *gangsas* create a single melodic line with pitches subdivided between them, interlocking in intricate rhythmic patterns, playing at rapid speed. From the beginning of the CD selection to 0:36 you can hear one of the two parts alone, from 0:36 to 1:03 the second part alone. From 1:03 to the end, the two parts join in a complete interlocking pattern (*kotekan*) to form the melody.

Rounds.   Along the continuum from horizontal to vertical orientation is the performance practice of singing a melody as a **round**. As you must know from singing rounds yourself, music makers begin the melody at systematically different spots, thereby overlapping. It is challenging, because you have to concentrate on singing the melody yourself—thinking horizontally—while at the same time hearing the combined voices vertically. The total effect can be so busy that one must listen carefully to be sure that just one melody is being rendered. On CD track 49, "Sumer is icumen in" is sung as a round from 0:36 to 1:34; in this performance the women start the round and the men join.

A melody sung as a round is just one type of a texture called **polyphony** (literally "multiple voices") in European music terminology (see further discussion below). When each singer imitates the melody of other singers (rather than simultaneously singing a different melody), the result is **imitative polyphony**. In a round (also called **canon**) the imitation is strict; everyone sings the melody just alike.

ACTIVITY 4.16 *Reach back in your memory for a round you sang when you were young. Try to sing that melody with a friend or group of friends—first in unison, then in multiple parts.*

Heterophony. In **heterophony** (literally "different voices") multiple musicians perform one melody, but each musician might render the melody somewhat differently. In Arab music, for example, a lute player and a flute player might give slightly different renditions of a melody, in part because of the idiomatic capabilities of each instrument. The flute player might insert frequent trills, or the lute player might insert rapid and repeated plucking of a single note. When played together, the two different renditions create a highly valued heterophonic texture (CD track 25).

Heterophony is widespread in Asian musical traditions. On CD track 51, the classical Japanese composition "Yaegoromo," the sung melody at the beginning is self-accompanied on *koto* and further accompanied on *syamisen* and *syakuhati* (figure 2.8). A heterophonic texture is created by the somewhat different pacing and pitches as the three instrumental parts and vocal combine to present "the melody."

ACTIVITY 4.17 *To test your hearing and understanding of different practices for performing a single melody, listen to these tracks on the CD and decide whether each is an example of monophony or heterophony: tracks 8, 12, 14, 18, 20, and 23.*

Performing One Melody with Another Part. A single melody can also be performed with one or more other parts that use pitch (as opposed to a nonpitched drum, for instance) but whose function is not melodic. Such a relationship among parts takes a number of forms in music throughout the world; I mention only two here.

Melody and Drone. A widespread manner of performing a single melody with a pitched but nonmelodic part is to put it over a **drone**. A drone is usually thought of as being one pitch that undergirds the melody by being sounded in a persistent fashion, as in Scottish bagpipe music (CD track 52).

However, there are multiple varieties of drone. On CD track 11, a short excerpt of North Indian *sitār* (plucked lute) music, the pitch *sa* is sounded intermittently on a string designated on the instrument for a drone; while the sounding of *sa* on that string is far from constant, its function is heard as a drone. A drone might also consist of multiple pitches. When the drone in India's music is kept on *tānpūra*, a chordophone devoted solely to that role, it consists of multiple pitches that are sounded in succession constantly from the beginning to the end of a performance selection (CD track 53). The metal strings of the *tānpūra* provide a lush sound quality that contrasts with the vocal timbre.

Homophony. Perhaps the most widespread practice of performing a single melody—thanks to the dissemination of American popular music worldwide—is to back it up with functional chords. The term for this texture is **homophony** (literally "same voice"). Chords undergird the melody, and the melody is conceived in terms of the harmony; in that sense, they are "the same voice." Because the term is so linked with tonal harmony, the label "homophony" is most applicable in such music. Examples can be heard on CD tracks 2, 6, 7, 21, 24, and others. In some homophonic music, such as choral renditions of hymns and patriotic songs, the harmonizing parts move in the same rhythm as the melody—another sense in which they are the "same voice."

Performing Multiple Melodies.
Polyphony. When multiple melodic parts are performed together, the texture is termed **polyphony** ("multiple voices"). The singing of rounds, the type of polyphony discussed above, is a musical practice in which one melody is taken up in turn by multiple musicians. Here, I discuss another type of polyphony; the texture achieved when multiple musicians perform different melodic parts simultaneously. But what constitutes a "melodic part"? Because they work with such a variety of

musical traditions, ethnomusicologists who want to use the term "polyphony" consider any number of things to be a melodic part—anything from a short ostinato to a full tune. In his volume on Bulgarian music in this series, Rice considers a two-part woman's song to be an example of polyphony: one woman sings "a melody" while the other sings a second melodic part, but not one he identifies as "a melody." Rice's idea of "melodic part" is typically flexible.

Melody and Ostinato.   Some scholars consider an **ostinato**—that is, a constantly recurring melodic, harmonic, or rhythmic motive—to be an extended form of drone.

A performance of "Sumer is icumen in" is not complete until the melody, which you have already heard performed in unison and as a round (CD track 49), is complemented by not one ostinato but two ostinati (called *pes* in medieval terminology). Each of them is a melodic motive. The text of ostinato 1 is "Sing cucu nu, sing cucu"; the text and melody of ostinato 2 reverse the two phrases: "Sing cucu, sing cucu nu." The two ostinati can be heard on CD track 49, from 1:28 to 1:57.

When all parts of "Sumer is icumen in" are performed together, a full polyphonic texture is created. From 2:01 to the end of CD track 49, you can hear the rich texture that results from the combination of the two ostinati and the melody performed as a three-part round. For performers and listeners, this piece demands simultaneous horizontal and vertical musical orientation.

In this chapter I have discussed pitch as the foundation for both melody and harmony, offering perspectives from music theory as well as practice. I also explored a variety of ways in which musical parts are made to relate. In the next chapter I shall discuss processes for structuring a musical selection.

CHAPTER 5

Thinking about Structure

∞

By **structure** I mean the shape of a musical selection, that is, its **form**. The topic of musical structure has arisen several times in earlier chapters: from the perspective of instruments in chapter 2, in the section "Ideas about Ensemble"; from the perspective of the organization of time in the second half of chapter 3; and from the perspective of texture in Chapter 4, in the section "Thinking Horizontally and Vertically." In this chapter I shall present several additional formal structures that musicians have found useful and meaningful.

Ethnomusicologists are interested in exploring not only *how* music is structured but also *why* it is structured the way it is. Accordingly, in this chapter I consider both structure as an element of music and structuring as a process in music making.

IMPROVISING AND COMPOSING

Pertinent to thinking about structures as things and structuring as a process is the ongoing lively discussion regarding what is encompassed by the two terms "improvisation" and "composition." That discussion has been particularly crucial in ethnomusicological study for several reasons. Much of the music discussed in this book involves the process of interweaving musical material that is given with material that is being newly created even as one listens. That process is generally called "improvising"; ethnomusicologists understand it also as "composing."

There are two misconceptions about improvisation that we in ethnomusicology have to counter regularly. One is that improvisation is completely "free," implying that music being newly created during performance is not based on anything preexisting. Ethnomusicological research has not confirmed that idea. Rather, we see musicians using something musical that already exists—an idea about ensemble relationships, a rhythm pattern, the pitch selection in a mode, or something else—as the basis for new music.

The other misconception is that improvisation is not composition—or, put another way, that the process of creating music during performance is intrinsically different from the process of creating music before a performance. This distinction involves a bundle of assumptions. First is the idea that the timing of the creative activity is crucial—that composing necessarily precedes performing. However, it is widely recognized now that composing is a cognitive process that can be taking place in the mind at any time—including while performing.

The idea that composing must precede performing accompanies the supposition that composing means writing something down (or, conversely, that if music is not written, it must be improvised). This interpretation does not take us far when we consider that much music is created in the world, but relatively few people are interested in notating it. For example, writing is not required for Indonesian musicians to remember enormously complex, lengthy compositions. (See Brinner 1995). In addition, notation systems are invented to suit the purposes of a particular musical tradition and may have little to do with what happens to the notated item when it is performed. (See "Transmission," in chapter 1.)

It is also sometimes assumed that the result of the compositional process is an item, a thing—a *piece*—which can be performed again and again in a relatively intact form. This idea about "a piece" is viable for a good deal of music, particularly if the modifier "relatively" is kept in mind: pieces in the European classical tradition, songs in the South Indian classical tradition, Anglo-American ballads, Mexican American *corridos*, and many other repertoires are transmitted in a relatively intact form. However, the corollary—that composing has not taken place if the process of creating music does not result in a relatively fixed product—is an assumption that ethnomusicologists do not find viable.

∽

The Ugandan musician Centurio Balikoowa, cited in Greg Barz's volume on East African music in this Global Music Series: "In most African musics we have this idea of the expectation and anticipation of the music always being developed within a performance. There is that idea that listening would be boring if we didn't continue to add things into the performance. When we have an ensemble of three endingidi, two will play in contrasting keys, while the third player will

*be expected to improvise and put in something different so
that they don't play the same thing."*

∞

More meaningful than defining in systematic ways what is "composed" and "improvised" is exploring the wide range of musical flexibility that exists in music around the world. The amount of flexibility and the nature of the flexibility that is exercised in the performance of given material varies widely from music to music. When an Anglo-American ballad or a Mexican American *corrido* is performed, the community expects some degree of change—but not too much—to occur in each performance; this results in recognizable variants and is known as "the folk process of re-creation," or "collective folk composition." Some flexibility—variations in phrasing, in speed, in dynamics perhaps—is expected in the performance of a good deal of notated music in the European classical tradition as well; this is called "interpretation." In a Middle Eastern ensemble performance, repetitions of precomposed music in the course of a performance are anticipated moments for variation, when the musicians are likely to add their own melodic ornaments or heterophonic realizations of the composed passages. In much music of Africa and the African diaspora, one primary structural principle assumes a particular form of flexibility—the contrast of something that varies with the more or less "fixed" patterns that make up a polyrhythmic texture.

Urged to define the term "improvisation," I suggest this. **Improvisation** is the result of a musician exercising relatively great flexibility with given material during a performance. The "given material" might be a tune, a chord progression, or a rhythm (twelve-bar blues or a drumming pattern), for example.

ACTIVITY 5.1 *Search your personal collection for recordings of two versions of one popular tune. Use those performances to analyze the degree of flexibility in the particular style of your selections. Think about the expectation for flexibility and the musical results. How would you define "composed music" in this context? Would you be tempted to call anything in the selection "improvisation"?*

And where does the idea of "an arrangement" fit in here?

PUTTING SOMETHING SIGNIFICANT FIRST

Easing gradually into a musical selection is a formal strategy that is preferred in a number of Asian musical genres. In North Indian classical music, a vocalist or instrumentalist will start a major selection in a formal concert by introducing the characteristics of the melodic mode (*rāga*) and establishing the mood through nonmetrical, carefully shaped improvisation called *ālāp* (CD tracks 11 and 53). The drummer in the ensemble, not yet playing, sits onstage listening; he is like a member of the audience, responding with a shake of the head or a quiet exclamation to particularly creative moments in the *ālāp*. The *rāga* provides the given material for an entire performance selection.

At the opposite extreme of easing into a piece of music is the clear announcement of an important motive right at the beginning.

> **ACTIVITY 5.2** *In European classical music, that opening motive is often the primary* **theme** *or subject matter of the entire piece. Try to identify two of the best-known beginnings in European classical music on CD tracks 40 and 54. If you recognize them, assist a classmate who does not.*

Though those two ways of beginning a selection are entirely different, they share a musical purpose crucial to the shaping of the whole selection: the most significant musical material is put first.

> **ACTIVITY 5.3** *Listen to the beginning of several selections by your favorite performing group or artist. Is there a consistent style for beginnings? If so, why, do you suppose? If not, why not, do you suppose?*

North Indian Instrumental Form. The beginning *ālāp* section asserts the primacy of melody in the hierarchy of music elements in the Hindustani tradition. In the most expansive musical form that comprises a performance selection of North Indian instrumental music (*ālāp-joṛ-*

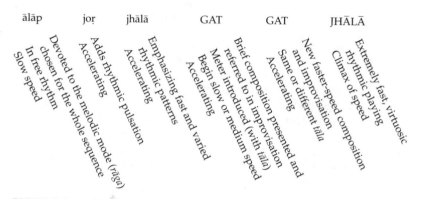

FIGURE 5.1 *Hindustani instrumental sequence.*

jhālā-gat-gat-jhālā), however, a gradual sequence occurs that systematically shifts focus to other elements of music (figure 5.1). Following the *ālāp*, the instrumentalist begins to add pulsating rhythm to the melodic improvisation (*joṛ*). Then, creating interesting rhythms with a combination of melody and drone pitches (*jhālā*), he or she accelerates the speed of the playing. The first real break in the sequence occurs as the drummer enters the selection; at that point a composition (*gat*) is presented, adding a metric cycle (*tāla*) and a tune in the *rāga* to the "given materials" that form the basis of further improvisation. The desire for gradual acceleration (see the section on speed in chapter 3) is turned into a structural principle when a composition in slow or medium speed is followed without break by a second composition in fast speed. This is a practice in Hindustani classical vocal music, as well.

Sonata Form. In many pieces in the European classical tradition, the opening theme is thoroughly *developed*—subjected to transformations that generate new musical ideas and moods—as the selection proceeds. One important form in European classical music in which that happens is **sonata form**. Sonata form features an opening section (A) that introduces one or more themes and includes a **modulation** to another key, a development of the themes in the middle section (B), and a return to the original key and recapitulation of the themes in the last section (A'; see figure 5.2). Developed by Viennese composers and used in almost all the first movements of their symphonies, sonatas, and other genres, sonata form became extremely significant in European classical music in the eighteenth and nineteenth centuries.

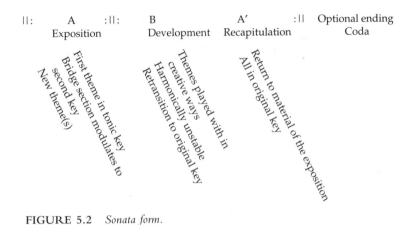

FIGURE 5.2 *Sonata form.*

Modulation, the shifting from one tonal center to another that is a crucial characteristic of sonata form, constitutes an important practice in structuring a good deal of music created in the tonal pitch system. As its occurence in "Marieke" (CD track 33) shows, it can be used to dramatic effect.

ACTIVITY 5.4 *Listen to CD track 33, "Marieke." A modulation occurs about three-quarters of the way through this performance. Can you identify when it happens? It will help to try to hear the tonic pitch through most of the song, then listen for a shift. Once you identify where it happens, try to articulate why it occurs where it does.*

TELLING THE STORY

In many instances the demands of telling a story musically are significant factors. In this section I offer a few examples of multiple responses to those demands.

Music for the Moment. As a *dalang* (puppeteer) in Indonesia weaves his story with shadow puppets, he sends cues to musicians who instantly respond with music appropriate for the moment—battle music, walking music, meditating music (figure 1.5). While the music with which they respond is pre-composed, the musicians cannot know in advance what will be called for when.

Part-Counterpart. Like the Indonesian *dalang,* the Liberian Kpelle epic pourer is completely in charge as he narrates the story of the hero Womi, a superhuman ritual specialist (CD track 55). The epic pourer voices all the parts, sings, responds to a volunteer questioner from the crowd, and directs a group of supporting listeners who also provide the musical backdrop. The structure within which he works is **part-counterpart**, in which one or more supporting parts responds to another part. In the Kpelle epic genre, that structure is played out in several ways simultaneously. Repeating what could have been one rhythmic part, two musical supporters tap bottles to form an interlocking rhythm. Another four or more young people form a chorus; what could have been one extended choral phrase is segmented between the two groups. The narrator and all the musicians together articulate a part-counterpart structure; the narrator's part is flexible, while the supporting group's parts are fixed. In addition, the narrator and the questioner articulate a part-counterpart structure; in that case, both parts are flexible.

Contrasting Instrumentation. In forms of music drama in numerous cultures, shifting instrumentation (including voices) is exploited fully. In the short section from the opera *Carmen* on CD track 21, the interplay among instruments, men's chorus, women's chorus, and heroine (Carmen) provides a kind of musical motion.

ACTIVITY 5.5 *Make a photocopy of the text given in Activity 4.7 and follow it as you listen again to CD track 21 to refresh your memory of the scene.*

Then focus your listening on the instrumentation. On the photocopied text, mark what you hear in terms of shifting instrumentation. Note who sings, with whom or alone, unaccompanied or accompanied, with what instrument, and the like. When you have completed your listening, write an analytical summary of the way Bizet uses instrumentation in structuring the scene.

FIGURE 5.3 *Tsun-yuen Lui playing Chinese* pipa. *(Courtesy of the UCLA Ethno-musicology Archives)*

Through-composed Music.   In "telling" the story of the battle in 202 B.C.E. between the monarch of the Ch'u dynasty and his challenger from what would become the Han dynasty in China, the music in "The Great Ambush" (CD track 56) continually changes. Because the musical content changes from beginning to end of the selection, the structure is called **through-composed**. Also, this particular example is programmatic, that is, an instrumental rendering of "a text." The piece opens with the *pipa* (figure 5.3) imitating the powerful and martial sound of drums in the high register; that is followed by highly dramatic effects produced by means of different playing techniques, speeds, **dynamics** (use of volume), and the like. Some of the music imitates sounds of a battlefield, while other passages only suggest thematic content.

ACTIVITY 5.6 *Listen to CD track 56, the first two minutes of "The Great Ambush" performed by Tsun-yuen Lui. Plot on a timing chart where the programmatic sections come in the piece in order to answer this question: Is the program clear, or not?*

Several versions of the program have been published, each listing the events of the battle. This one suggests eighteen sections: massing of troops, the line up, drum beats, the signals, artillery barrage, bugle calls to open a gate, calling the generals, taking battle stations, the dispatch, the ambush, the skirmish, the cannonade, shouts, the charge, the siege, the call to retreat, the Ch'u army routed, the suicide of the Ch'u leader.

Strophic Form. **Strophic form** provides an excellent structure for telling a story. The word "strophe" (stanza or verse) usually refers to the text, but it has been adapted in musical terminology to refer to a song tune that is repeated while the text changes. That is the form chosen for *corridos*. The melody of "The Ballad of César Chávez" (CD track 7; figure 1.4) is strophic: the same melody is repeated for each stanza of text.

	Text lines	Melody lines
Verse 1	A B C D	A B C D
Verse 2	E F G H	A B C D
Verse 3	I J K L, etc.	A B C D, etc.

ACTIVITY 5.7 *The selections on CD track 24 "Take Five," and CD track 32 "West End Blues," are both in strophic form, though their "verses" or "stanzas" are called "choruses." Make a listening chart for each, in which you articulate what changes and what stays the same. Return to earlier discussions of them for some guidance.*

The historic 1914 calypso "Iron Duke in the Land," by Julian Whiterose, stretches the strophic form with the addition of a **refrain** or

chorus (CD track 57). Whereas in a strophe only the melody repeats, in a refrain or chorus both the text and melody repeat. Whiterose sings the chorus twice at the outset, and then repeats it after each verse. Its recurrence dramatizes the sarcasm in the text; this is commentary on a situation so well known to listeners that there is no need to tell the story. The ending phrase "sans humanité" is a reminder of the early days of staged calypso song duels. Whether or not songs were about fighting and confrontation, it remained common practice throughout the 1920s and 1930s to sing the phrase "without pity" (Shannon Dudley, in the volume on Trinidad in this series).

Whenever so much repeats, it is advisable to listen for what is changing musically. In this particular strophic song it is the rhythm of the text setting in the verses that changes, causing phrase lengths to be irregular.

IRON DUKE IN THE LAND
Chorus
Iron Duke in the land
Fire brigade
Iron Duke in the land
Fire brigade, bring the locomotive
Just because it's a fire federation
Bring the locomotive
Just because it's a fire federation
Sans humanité!

Verse 1
Remember ? ? '95
When I was a teacher and Lord Adulator
They called to me two years later
As Second Lord and then Advocator
Advocator, they called me Advisor,
Was Advisor and now Supervisor
Me name Supervisor, and they call me Lord
*   of this island*
? ? devirey [return]

Verse 2 [The singer bragging of his prowess]
At my appearance upon the scene
Julius the devil played the Cord
And still I am the head of fraternal order
Calling, sweeping to all the agony

Achieving my surprising majesty
In blending, beaming and swaying
Jumping this way, bawling, "clear de way,
    Whiterose joli
Djable ré-ré-o" [Handsome Whiterose, the
    devil king]

Verse 3
It was a modern manifestation
Of the elder civilization
That muh carnival celebration
Of this social organization
It call-ed to mind to an abstention [misusing fancy English]
Over all the population
I, Julian, taking the social decor, deh who whey, [they who wear the
    uniform, masquerade or emblem of]
    Whiterose Union
Sans humanité.

RESPONDING TO THE CONTEXT

In many instances, musical selections are structured in response to something in the context, broadly conceived. The short time available on early recordings, for instance, caused musicians to curtail what would have been longer selections. Composing for a particular opera diva causes a score to have more arias for one character than others. If a cathedral has balconies on either side from which choirs might sing or instrumentalists might play, a composer might write interactive music to surround the worshipers with affective sound. Below, I sample a few contexts to demonstrate this point further.

Expectation for Audience-Performer Interaction.   In an improvised performance such as the Hindustani performance sequence described in figure 5.1, audience response can play a big part in how the soloing musician proportions the music he or she is creating. If the audience notes approval with "wah! wah!" or with a shake of the head, then the musical idea that drew the response might get prolonged, repeated with subtle changes.

    Audience-performer interaction can also shape performances by some larger groups such as the Middle Eastern ensemble on CD track 25 (figure 5.4). Arab audiences react in the moment; this performer-

Muqaddima (Ensemble introduction) - - - - - - - - - - - - - - - - - - -Song

Rubato section - - - - - - - - - - - -Section in rhythmic mode - - - -Song
    (rhythmic ebb & flow)   (from 1:28)   (at 3:02)
Full ensemble, followed by   Full ensemble
Qanun solo with ensemble   Melody played 5 times, at
    responses (from 0:58)   1:27, 1:46, 2:02, 2:19,
                                       2:35
                                 Ending phrase repeated
                                     quietly as transition

FIGURE 5.4 *Egyptian performance structure.*

audience feedback system ideally involves an upward spiraling process in which everyone "gets high." The lively interaction can be heard at several points even in the short portion of a selection reproduced in CD track 25: at the beginning, during the *rubato* section (to 1:27), and beyond.

The Need for Intra-ensemble Interaction. Intra-ensemble interaction is at play in the selection on CD track 25 from 1:28, when the full ensemble launches into a melody in rhythmic mode. The number of repetitions of that melody will depend on the context; in this instance it is played five times. As the ensemble performs this precomposed introduction, the singer, Umm Kulthum, would traditionally be sitting in a chair in the center of the ensemble semicircle. When she is ready to sing, she stands up; on CD track 25 that happens during the fourth time through the melody (between 2:19 and 2:35), and you can hear the audience responding with applause. Her ensemble, understanding her signal that it is time to move on in the composition, responds by softening its sound a little. But in this performance, she must not have been quite ready to start singing. Seeing her signal that unreadiness with her hand, the *qanun* player (the leader of her ensemble) must have signaled to everyone else because we hear the ensemble energized. It repeats the melody again. The whole introduction (*muqaddima*) ends with a small phrase played quietly over and over so that focus shifts fully to the singer. Everyone waits, as she decides when the mood is right to begin singing.

Now the audience-performer interaction intersects with intra-ensemble interaction. Umm Kulthum sings the first phrase of the song "Aruh li min" (at 3:02), and the audience responds with a huge wave of applause. So strong is the applause that she stops singing. She has stopped for at least two reasons: she needs to acknowledge the applause, and she also needs to make sure that she does not lose control of the crowd. Whenever the audience response got "over the top," Umm Kulthum would stop and politely wait for the audience's energy to dissipate. Toward her audience she was respectful and appreciative but always in control. What do the ensemble players do? They keep playing, but they have not yet figured out what to do. Their interaction with the singer continues as they await the signal to proceed (Scott Marcus, personal communication, 2001).

In this one selection of Egyptian music, then, we see that the precomposed piece has a set structure (a *rubato* section that includes space for an elaborating *qanun* solo, a full ensemble section in rhythmic mode, and a song), but the execution of that structure in performance is shaped by the musicians, responding in a flexible manner to cues from the audience and from each other.

A Ritual Context.   When an Indian or Pakistani *qawwālīyā* sings in a Muslim Sufi gathering, he watches the participants for signs of going into trance in order to encourage it musically; the ritual process and a devotional response structure the music (Qureshi 1987). The shaping of music in response to a ritual situation happens all over the world.

A Series of Changdan.   Revealing their origin in shamanistic ritual, several concert performance genres of Korean music use a progression through a series of *changdan* as the single most important structuring principle (see chapter 3). Effecting a gradual buildup of tension that is reminiscent of the progress of a ritualized seance (*kut*), the rhythm patterns change in a series of sections. That is the structure of the important solo instrumental genre of *sanjo* (CD track 17). Not only does the rhythm pattern change, but the speed of the basic beats also gets gradually faster from the beginning to the end of a piece.

ACTIVITY 5.8   *Track the succession of* changdan *through the selection on CD track 17, portions of a solo instrumental performance genre called* sanjo. *Here it is played on* komúngo *by*

Han Kap-deuk *(figure 2.13) and, on* chang-gu, *by* Hwang
Deuk-ju. *Note the gradual increase in speed.*
Chinyangjo changdan *(through three and one-half times: sec-*
ond time at 0:53, third time at 1:38, fourth time at 2:19)
(24) • - - - - - - - - - - • - - - • • | • - - - - - - - - - - - •
   - - • - - • |
• - - - - - - - - - - - - • - - - • - | • - - - - - - - - - - •
   - - • - - • ||
2:42 Chungmori begins
(12) • - - - - - - - • - - - • - - - • • - - - - - - • - - - • - - -
   - - - - • - - - |
4:53 Onmori *begins (fade-out at 5:00)*
(10)

∞

It is Sunday morning at the Power of Jesus Around the World
Church located along the outskirts of Kisumu, Kenya.... The
congregation is invited to begin the service by laying their
hands on a group of members who recently lost a family mem-
ber. Before long, one of the service's leaders begins to speak
in tongues. The bereaved members all fall to the ground as
they too begin proclaiming in unintelligible statements. Within
minutes a large portion of the congregation is swept up in the
spirit and the emotion of the moment. . . . After an extended
period of time one of the pastors begins the call of a well-
known chorus known in North America as "Kumbaya" [CD
track 58], singing into a generator-powered microphone. The
give and take between the soloist and the congregation builds
up gradually. The spirit healing session "cools" down after a
half hour or so, and the performance of "Kumbaya" reunites
the community, giving them back "language" while at the
same time bringing them back to their seats. (Greg Barz, in
the volume on East Africa in this series)

∞

Call and Response.   The musical structure in the Kenyan religious service described by Greg Barz—**call and response**—is sometimes taken generally to imply the juxtaposition of solo with group, sometimes more pointedly referring to a musical repartee among parts. In either case, it is deeply significant in African music: the master drummer or singer who creates one part to which an ensemble of instrumentalists or singers respond, the xylophone duo in which one player leads and the other responds, the praise singer whose listeners encourage him or her with a response. Transported to North America in the era of slavery, that structure could be heard as one worker led in song, with fellow workers responding; in contemporary gospel a lead singer embellishes a solo with support from the choir; in the blues there is the same sort of interplay between singer and instrumentalists as well among the instrumentalists. Transported to South America and retained in musical practices, there it forms, for instance, the structure of the Brazilian *capoeira* selection on CD track 59.

ACTIVITY 5.9   *The structures of solo-group instrumentation and musical part-counterpart is heard in music all over the world. With that idea as a focus, review the variety of musical practices that are offered on the CD. Listen to each selection again, for the purpose of finding those structures.*

Music and Movement.   In the forefront of *capoeira*, a Brazilian street game (now institutionalized), is coordination in structuring music along with physical play. On CD track 59 singer and chorus do a call and response, with an ensemble of *berimbau* (a musical bow), *pandeiro* (tambourine), *agogô* (double metal bell, hard to hear), *reco-reco* (notched bamboo scraper), and *atabaque* (large drum resembling a conga) forming the now-familiar polyrhythmic backdrop. Competing within a circle of spectators, two contestants use athletic leg thrusts to throw each other off balance. As physical play changes, the music should change accordingly, and if the music changes, the contestants should respond in kind. "The musicians [all *capoeristas* themselves] create the atmosphere within which the game comes to life; they make the game possible, and the game, in turn, gives meaning to the music" (Lewis 1992: 134).

When music is meant for dance, it is important to coordinate the form of the music and the dance. Thousands of Irish dance tunes have a **binary form**—A and B sections (CD track 37). Each section is eight measures long. The two sections are usually repeated in performance, creating a tune that is thirty-two measures long.

> **ACTIVITY 5.10** *On CD track 37, "Tar Road to Sligo" is played for one minute and thirty-one seconds before the musicians move on to the second jig ("Paddy Clancy's") in a medley. The band consists of fiddle (Becky Tracy), mandolin (Stan Scott), and whistle (Dora Hast). The tunes move in compound duple meter at a fast clip. The first section (A) is repeated exactly. The B section varies the pattern a bit: In the repeat, the first four measures are retained exactly, but the last four measures are slightly different (B'). The total structure is: A A B B' A A B B' A A B B', with each segment taking about eight seconds.*
>
> *Listen to CD track 37 and identify what changes, in the midst of so much repetition.*

The bipartite structure of dance tunes in the British Isles and in associated traditions in North America are closely linked to the structures of the dances. Many Irish, Scottish, and English set formation dances feature a setting section (dancers remaining in place) followed by a traveling part. Anyone who has participated in North American square dances will recognize this structure: one section of the tune is used when the active couple dances a figure with another couple in the square, then returns to place; the second section corresponds with the promenade or traveling part. The influence of dance structure on the performance of dance tunes can still be heard when the tunes are played in a listening context such as a concert or a *seisun* (session) like those described in the Scott-Hast volume on Irish music in this series (figure 5.5). The structure of tunes remains the same, but the tunes are grouped in different kinds of medleys, as in CD track 37, to maintain musical interest without the dance (Peggy Duesenberry, personal communication, 2001).

FIGURE 5.5 *Session at Gleeson's of Coore, near Miltown Malbay Co. Clare. The session has been a feature for decades, catering to musicians and dancers alike. In this photo the musicians are Ita Crehan (keyboard), Eamonn McGivney (fiddle), Conor Keane (accordeon), Michael Downes (fiddle), P. J. Crotty (flute, mostly hidden), Angela Crotty-Crehan (concertina). The set dancers include singer Peggy McMahan and singer/concertina player Kitty Hayes. Musicians Junior Crehan and Annette Munelly are having a break at the bar.* (© Peter Laban, Miltown Malbay Co. Clare)

COMING TO THE END

The musical term for an ending is **cadence**. "Cadence" encompasses not only what happens at the very end but also how the ending is approached. The use of speed is another possible practice for coming to closure. Listening again to "Marieke" (figure 3.3, CD track 33), you can hear how acceleration is used to approach the ending. In a good deal of music, slowing down occurs to mark the ending.

In most tonal music the ending is a matter of harmonic practice: we expect the last chord to be the tonic chord. The *corrido* and blues selections (CD tracks 7 and 32) demonstrate this cadential practice clearly. There is also a common practice in the choice of chords that lead up to the tonic and cause us to expect the ending. In the *corrido* and blues and in a great deal of other tonal music, the V (dominant) chord will immediately precede the tonic. Melodically, in tonal music pitch 7 (*ti*) or 2 (*re*) often functions as a lower or upper leading tone respectively, causing us to expect resolution to the tonic pitch.

Musical practice for creating an ending might involve rhythm and the metric structure. In North Indian improvisational practice, musical units will usually end on a count 1. Because the improvising musician could decide to stop at any count 1 and needs to signal the accompanists to create an ending simultaneously, musical cues must be sounded leading up to that ending on count 1. One type of cue is a *tihāī*—a melodic or rhythmic pattern that is performed three times, with the last repetition ending on the cadential count 1.

Especially when music is structured in response to a fluid context, consideration of cadential practice (i.e., how something ends) needs to be complimented by considering why the music is brought to an end. The story is finished, the performance time runs out, the artist is ready to quit, the audience loses interest, the person in trance returns to consciousness—all these and more can bring about musical ending.

ACTIVITY 5.11 *Listen to at least three musical selections of your choice. Analyze and articulate how the ending is created and consider why.*

AESTHETIC CHOICE AND INTELLECTUAL PLAY

The aesthetic values held by people about music constitute one of the most meaningful of contexts. Any number of musical forms can be understood as results of aesthetic and intellectual decisions. Here are two examples.

Contrasting Rhythmic Modes. In Middle Eastern music, with its systems of melodic modes and rhythmic modes, the deep value placed on the power of music to express mood is seen in aspects of musical form. One of those is the juxtaposition of different rhythmic modes. As composed by Riyad al-Sinbati, the selection on CD track 25 is in *maqsum* rhythmic mode beginning at 1:28. Contrasting with that, the song (3:02, just as the track ends) starts in *wahdah* rhythmic mode: Dumm – – Takk – – Takk –. The composer's reason is a change of mood, as *wahdah* is weightier and more appropriate for a serious song. Marcus features this song in his volume on Middle Eastern music in this series.

Contrasting Melodic Modes. Intellectual play as well as aesthetic choice are the major factors in an improvisatory South Indian performance practice called *rāgamālikā* ("garland of ragas"). *Rāgamālikā* comprises a progression from one *rāga* to another, each sufficiently similar that one must listen closely to detect the shift, but sufficiently different that contrast has been achieved. The intellectual play is enhanced when, in vocal *rāgamālikā*, the names of the new modes are introduced into the text, embedded in clever ways.

SOCIAL VALUES

In this chapter, I have taken the ethnomusicological approach of exploring not only *how* music is structured but also *why* it might be structured the way it is. To end, I shall demonstrate how one social value held by different groups of people is played out musically in different ways. The shared value is this: the conduct of cooperative, supportive social relationships within a group is prized above individual achievement.

As observed by Santosa and cited in chapter 2, the Central Javanese tradition of *gamelan* music (CD track 8) is a practice that conserves relations not only among patrons and the musicians but also among members of the community; it is a communal practice in which no one individual stands out. This can be heard in the homogeneous nature of the sound ideal. Furthermore, no one instrumental part stands out from the others in any sustained manner; the marking of the important colotomic structure on multiple instruments is embedded in the ensemble melody. Even in the modal introduction, the one section of a piece in which a single "voice" might be heard as an individual, the constraints of brevity and conventional instrumental patterns keep the expression of individual musicality in check. The music expresses community.

Jazz, in comparison, is a musical practice that, above all others, symbolizes throughout the world the African American identity that emerged from within difficult human circumstances. Even when jazz is practiced by people of other groups—as it is, all over the globe—its meaning is remembered and resignified (CD tracks 24 and 36). Performance practice in jazz is of a group, for a group, expressing a cause held in common or remembering that cause. Rather than submerging the individual musicians within the group in the musical structure, however, individual creativity is featured in two ways—cooperatively, in that individual players take the spotlight in turn, and competitively, as musicians engage in fierce cutting contests that display and stretch their explicitly jazz-style musicianship. Through musical practice, a global musical community is created even as the historical and culturally-specific senses of community continue.

In this chapter I have discussed how and why the structuring of music contributes to making music meaningful and useful in people's lives. Aspects of earlier discussions—of instruments in ensembles, of rhythmic, of melodic and harmonic practice—have been recycled, to put the pieces together, in a manner of speaking. In the final two chapters, I shift the focus explicitly to ethnomusicology as an intellectual field and research practice.

CHAPTER 6

Thinking about Issues

∞

When the moment came to write this chapter, I was in French Polynesia, following the lure of the South Pacific to celebrate a significant birthday. In this beautiful place, I wondered, how can I concentrate on writing about the topics that unify the case studies in this series—such matters as globalization, identity, and authenticity? I need not have worried, for the issues were all around me. Globalization, for instance: the music that newly made Polynesian friends wanted me to send them upon my return home was American—ranging from rock 'n' roll and rhythm and blues to the latest styles. By no means, they said, was American popular music meant to replace "their own" music; it was just that the global availability of American music presented a range of choices. I, on the other hand, especially wanted to experience "their music," something different that would permit me a glimpse even as a tourist of another culture. And, frankly, as an ethnomusicologist with a historical bent, I wanted to reassure myself that the cries of alarm heard for years over inevitable "gray-out," or homogenization, of the world's cultures in the face of unmitigated global flow had not erased the beautiful Polynesian music that is audible on recordings distributed in the United States. I need not have been so concerned; "the local" lives on.

What I had not really focused on before I got to Tahiti was that it is *French* Polynesia. French Polynesia is not a nation-state; its residents have voted to continue its status as a territory although it is thousands of miles from France. Tahiti's political status serves as a reminder of the long era of colonialism, when European nations (and relatively more recently, the United States and Japan) asserted claims over a substantial portion of the earth. Colonialism forms the backdrop for numerous new nation-states and the sense of nationalism therein. Here around me, I now realized, were the ever lively topics of the nature and effects of culture contact and the formation of senses of identity and relations of power—all topics important in the study of music.

In this chapter I shall discuss a selection of those topics, but first a commentary on two rubrics is needed: "music in global culture" and "world music." "Global culture" suggests that there are ideas, systems of production, and products circulating among peoples to the extent that something is widely shared. As one reader of this book in manuscript form put it, in the twenty-first century there are no completely isolated musical communities any longer; something connects all musical production and permits music to be simultaneously global and local: global in its production, distribution, and consumption by audiences, while local in its performance aesthetic and situatedness in a coherent cultural milieu. Tahitian music can then claim cultural space anywhere it is listened to (likewise American popular music), but its place is still an island in French Polynesia. "There's a sense that geography doesn't have to equal destiny. . . . Many new global artists have the curiosity to wander the earth with their music and the integrity to stay connected to their homelands" (Farley 2001: 7).

The rubric "world music" was first coined (as far as I know) by ethnomusicologists in the early 1960s to categorize instruction in traditions other than those of European classical music. It became an industry-sponsored term, a convenient label for the marketing of those traditional musics. "The most exhaustive guide to them, *World Music: The Rough Guide*, looks at 'ethnic' musics in particular places; here, the editors are concerned mainly with what they perceive to be 'indigenous,' 'authentic' musics. And they are marketing their book primarily to those western consumers who want to buy what they believe to be the authentic, the real" (Taylor 1997: 16).

In time, "world music" came to include popular music produced around the world. The term had always carried the sense of "Other," and the rubric "world beat" took on the same connotation. In his 1997 book *Global Pop*, Tim Taylor points out that while "world music" and "world beat" are putatively labels for musics, they are more often used to label musicians: "If it seems that the world beat category refers to music that is somehow exotic, different, fresh, and North American/British pop/rock oriented, it is also true that musicians who make this— or any—music that sounds mainstream will be categorized by their ethnicity rather than music" (16–17). Writing for *Time*, Christopher Farley asserts: "The old-school term world music is a joke, a wedge, a way of separating English-language performers from the rest of the planet. But there has always been crossover . . . in 1967 Frank Sinatra recorded an album of songs by Brazilian composer Antonio Carlos (Tom) Jobim. . . .

Such music became world music only when darker-skinned folks sang it" (2001: 7).

It is, I think, time for us to move on from the term "world music." The title "Global Music Series" for this set of textbooks is intended to encompass the study of music as it flourishes in some places in the globalized contemporary world—whether that music springs from a particular long tradition or results from global interaction.

Scholarly discussions of globalization speak of it in terms of processes that transcend boundaries of various sorts—national, ethnic, racial, class, gender, stylistic, and others: processes that are causing us to reconsider the nature of culture contact; causing musicians to challenge senses of ownership of cultural property and concepts of authenticity; and fostering hybridization and synthesis. To contextualize globalization, I shall step back and trace some roots, the backdrop to the condition of music in the twenty-first century.

MUSIC AND CULTURE CONTACT

From the earliest days of ethnomusicology in American universities, music has been studied through the lives of people. The first work was undertaken from the 1920s by scholars trained in anthropology and located in tribal cultures—primarily American Indian and also African. Ethnographical studies by Alice Fletcher, Helen Roberts, George Herzog, David McAllester, Alan Merriam, and others explored how music functioned for groups and interpreted repertoires as reflections of values and social structures. As the field has developed, numerous scholars have written about the processes of and responses to contact between groups with different music.

A Focus on Influences. Having witnessed considerable change in the musical traditions of the groups they studied, anthropologists in the 1930s developed a theory of change, termed "acculturation." In 1961 a statement of the theory was carefully crafted: "Acculturation comprehends those phenomena which result when groups of individuals having different cultures come into sustained first-hand contact, with subsequent changes in the original culture patterns of either or both groups" ("Criteria for Acculturation," 1961). Specific elements of that statement should be noted: individuals within groups are credited; the nature of the contact being considered is first-hand (i.e., not mediated) and sustained; and change might result for either one or both groups. Unfortunately, the term "acculturation" became applied to studies that skewed this theory: Groups became lumps of people (whole tribes or immigrant groups). Furthermore, the change that was noted in acculturation studies was primarily in the culture of subaltern groups, as the theorists belonged to what was perceived as and was in reality a dominant group (as in "the West" and "the rest"). A habit developed of essentializing the culture of whole groups—that is, citing one or a set of traits that one can easily forget are enormous generalizations, sometimes with historical political roots, such as the biologically racialized assertion that all Africans have a good sense of rhythm.

A Focus on Boundaries. The introduction by Fredrick Barth to a collection of essays titled *Ethnic Groups and Boundaries: The Social Organisation of Culture Difference* (1969) contributed to a shift of scholarly focus from acculturation—the influence of one group on another—to the construction and maintenance of boundaries between people. The term "ethnic group" was introduced, reflecting the anthropological concern with classification (Stokes 1994: 6). Significantly, this meant a shift to greater inclusiveness: rather than viewing culture mostly from the perspective of a dominant group, all groups were potentially given voices by analysis of social action, called "social performance" by the French theorists Pierre Bourdieu (1977) and M. de Certeau (1984). Ethnomusicologists began exploring musical practices as evidence of people's using music in the construction and maintenance of boundaries between themselves and other groups. Whether the Other is a dominant group or another subaltern group, a large proportion of these studies focus on relations of power among peoples. Many studies have appeared under the rubric of "identity study," that is, the examination of musical practices that express, if not assert, difference through the construction of an identity of some sort—gender, national, ethnic, individual, class, age, or some other. In the following sections, I explore those senses of groupness and identity that emerge as significant in several of the case study volumes in this series.

Gender. Studies that focus on gender are about the ways maleness and femaleness are constructed. (Gender is a cultural category, while sexuality is a biological category.) Concerning gender, you can find observations scattered throughout this book; in chapter 2, for instance, I explore the gendering of some musical instruments.

Historically in ethnomusicological writing, as in other scholarly disciplines, gender has usually gone unnoted unless the musical practice being studied is particularly associated with females. Otherwise, maleness is taken for granted, and male spheres of cultural action have received the lion's share of attention. Focus on women and their musical practices is burgeoning, however, expecially in the form of studies of individual musicians (Danielson 1997, for instance) and of particular groups of women (Sugarman 1997 and Koskoff 2001, for example). A variety of perspectives are being taken—woman musicians as symbols of a nation, as players of gendered roles in a community, as forces for social or cultural change, as political spokespersons, as culture bearers, and as individual artists. Ideally, whether the focus of our study is musicking by males or females, and particularly when the focus is on both, we should remark on gender because of its many implications for understanding musical practice. Further examples of gender and music I present here are drawn from the case studies in this textbook series.

Performance in public by females has been a thorny issue in many places. Women who brave the possible consequences of having their music received as performed sexuality rather than expressive artistry have been pioneers. In Middle Eastern cultures, for instance, the respectability of a female performer must be carefully negotiated; the stardom of a singer such as Umm Kulthum in Egypt is quite remarkable in light of that reality (CD track 25). In both South and North India female vocalists of classical genres have in the past found the refusal to accept payment for performance as a means of maintaining unquestionable respectability. Performances on radio—heard but not seen—presented a new and respectable context for women singers.

In so many instances, the performance of a particular musical genre is a gender role. Exploring the reasons for that can reveal much about the culture and its history. In Japan, for instance, the musico-dramatic form *kabuki* has been performed exclusively by males for several centuries, although it originated with female performance. In America women instrumentalists still find it difficult to break into the predominantly male world of jazz instrumental performance.

The control of musical knowledge is another arena where gender considerations often arise. In India, whether the learners are male or female, most teachers have been men. In contemporary Japan, while there are a few famous male performers of *koto*, instruction on the instrument has passed almost entirely into the purview of women (Figure 2.8).

Likewise, the authoritative role of leader in musical ensembles is often subject to gender considerations. North American women are making their way increasingly into the ranks of professional choral conductors (figure 1.1). In the orchestral world, however, the gender barriers are tall and thick; there are still few professional women orchestral conductors.

Ideas about masculinity and femininity can be understood by considering the matter of performance style. American women's groups in the 1960s adopted the Bulgarian women's choral sound—powerful, loud, and direct—as a means of expressing a new way of being female, a way that in American culture at that time suggested masculinity.

Conversely, it is important to note when the gender of a performer is explicitly not the point. In China, the manner in which gender is represented in musical drama is more important than the actual gender of the performer. The dramatic role of a refined woman, for instance, may be played by either a woman or a man, with the same expectations for sound quality and presentation. Likewise, in Javanese dance, the representation of the idea of refinement is most important, whether the dancer is male or female; it is character that is portrayed by the performance style, not gender. In some traditional Japanese vocal music, it is difficult to tell whether a man or a woman is singing, so ungendered is the style; an expressive rendering of the text is the most important criterion for performance style.

Culture change with regard to gender and music has become a prominent issue in research. The emergence of a star system in the past two decades in many places appears to be changing the situation for women musicians. While a female Javanese singer (*pesindhen*) in non-*gamelan* contexts may perform in a style with prominent overtones of sexuality, in the context of *gamelan* she must mask those overtones (CD track 8). Cultural knowledge of the association of the *pesindhen* and sexuality, however, makes her presence ever intriguing, and her status is rising. At present in Indonesia, the amount of attention that should be accorded her is a dilemma.

The National Community.   The clearest boundaries between groups are those of nations. A great deal of attention has been focused on expressions of national identity, with music playing important roles. The word "nation" is used in two senses. In the sense of culture, the term "nation" is applied to some subgroups within a geopolitical nation—American Indian nations and an African American nation being two examples. (See Adelaida Reyes's case study on the United States in this series.) In the geopolitical sense, the term "nation" is applied to an independent political area with geographic boundaries. The term "nation-state" adds to that latter sense the state, an apparatus for management, a mechanism for the maintenance of an internal community and the conduct of relations with other nations. The modern nation-state as a political reality came into being in Europe in the eighteenth century and gathered momentum with world events in the nineteenth and early twentieth centuries.

Nation-states developed as the site for processes of modernization, wherein the growth of the capitalist economic system spawned urbanization, the commercialization of culture, and the intensified use of technology as in industrialization. To consolidate and communicate changing values, public school systems were instituted, and the use of mass media for communication expanded as a basic tool. European and then North American processes of modernization then served as the model for the rest of the world, synonymous with "progress" and deemed inevitable in evolutionary terms.

A basic component of the economic success of the modern European nation-states was the extension of their geographical boundaries for political control of a substantial amount of the world's land and population. As the tools of modernization were applied in colonized areas, they became coupled with the inexorable influence of Western culture on Others. In the cultural sphere this could mean, for instance, instruction in European music in new public school systems and the transmission of music through the media of the new music industries. The case study by Marcus on music in the Middle East considers westernization and modernization in relation to contexts for music making, instruments and ensembles, attitudes toward music, music in the schools, and pedagogy.

Asserting the superiority of music of "the West" was a component of modernizing. "Drawing on earlier social-evolutionist theory which defined the 'modern' industrialized countries (civilization) as the present and 'traditional' societies (the savage and barbarian stages) as the past, the discourse of modernity defines itself as the all-encompassing present and future, and all alternatives ('the traditional') as an outmoded past" (Turino 2000: 6–7).

Belief in the superiority of European music—a legacy of the colonial era—has been deeply endorsed in some countries that were colonized or, like Japan, otherwise had to deal with the power of "the West." Japanese leaders invested in that opinion in their process of modernizing in the nineteenth century and transmitted it to Koreans, whom they colonized in the early twentieth century. The dilemma this assertion has caused for musicians of indigenous traditions in those countries is serious and ongoing. The situation in Japan and Korea is quite striking when compared to that of India: political leaders and musicians alike in that former jewel in the crown of the British empire have been unswervingly confident of the superiority of their classical music, with its long history, intellectuality, and spirituality. In India, classical music's greatest challenge is in the marketplace and is posed by music for the behemoth film industry that began to emerge during the colonial period.

The critique of westernization, meaning "the spread of Northwestern, Euro-American ideas, values, political organizations, and technologies," was a component in one early discourse (discussion adhering to a certain rationale) on globalization as well as in the discourse on modernization. "In that discourse, colonizing countries are referred to as the agents of globalization, and ethnomusicologists' work was focused on the dichotomy that such a framework had created: either the study of the Westernization of the local or, conversely, the local resistance to Westernization" (Guilbault: forthcoming). In both cases, a typically Western way of thinking in polarities was established in popular music studies: global versus local, the West and the rest. Precedents were in place, however.

Culture contact in the course of colonizing the Middle East and India had given rise to a discourse about "the Occident" and "the Orient," adhering to a rationale that Edward Said termed "orientalism." In Said's words, orientalism is "a system of knowledge about the Orient, an accepted grid for filtering through the Orient into Western consciousness" (1978: 6), a "cultural enterprise, a project whose dimensions take in such disparate realms as the imagination itself . . . the spice trade, colonial armies . . . a complex array of 'Oriental' ideas (Oriental despotism, Oriental splendor, cruelty, sensuality), many Eastern sects, philosophies, and wisdoms domesticated for local European use" (1978: 4). Lest we associate this discourse only with the British and French who dominated "the Orient" from the early nineteenth century until the end of World War II, Said reminds us that since that time America has dominated the Middle East and approaches it (and East Asia also) as France and Britain once did. In chapter 4 I examined a microscopic manifestation of orientalism—"the Oriental scale," with its lingering reference to sensual Otherness.

World War II (1941–45) effectively disrupted the paradigm of global (imperial) colonialism; a number of new nations came into being in the ensuing decades. Several independent nations also emerged near the end of the twentieth century from the dissolution of the Soviet Union. Not surprisingly, nation building—and therefore music and nationalism—is a topic that persists in ethnomusicological study.

Processes other than modernization and westernization also are at work in nation building. Among them are the construction of a united community, the choosing of emblems of representation that all citizens may share, and the assertion of some sort of difference by which one nation-state can be distinguished from others. Music can be important in each of them. To demonstrate these processes, I shall continue to move between historical and present time and continue to draw on case studies in this series for examples.

One of the first tasks in building a new nation-state is to create a united community—an "imagined community" (Anderson 1991)—even when the population is heterogeneous in some way. In French Polynesia the diversity is ethnic, with Tahitians and multigenerational resident Chinese, Japanese, Europeans, and Americans. In addition, the territory's several islands have long traditions of distinguishing themselves from each other. If French Polynesia were to become a nation-state, it would need to deal with the inevitable claims of multiple groups and construct a national identity.

For colonial Americans of the eighteenth century, the new identity could not be an outgrowth of shared language, beliefs, customs, traditions, and norms the way it was in European nation-states. Americanists point out that the United States may be the only nation in the world that was invented from an idea, lacking any foundation in a defined territory, a religious authority, a common culture, or a single people. Indeed, the Indian tribes, the country's earliest inhabitants, were themselves separate nations, each with a language and culture of its own. Until 1871, when congressional action ended the practice, those nations, their sovereignty recognized, could separately negotiate treaties with the U.S. government. These political conditions, combined with the multiplicity of cultures that Indian nations represented, made it highly unlikely that support for an overall American national identity might have been constructed on an Indian tribal base. (See Reyes's case study on the United States for further discussion.)

From the 1870s the Japanese government found Western music useful for nation building. Once they made the decision to follow the European and American model for including music in their new public education system (established expressly as a tool in the modernization process), they faced a dilemma: the various indigenous traditional genres had such deep class and other type of group associations that none could satisfy the community-building task for which music was needed. The solution was to adopt a different (i.e., non-Japanese) music that could be transmitted in such a way that it would be shared by all Japanese. As a result of the continuing emphasis on European music for over 130 years, Japan's traditional music has become exotic to most of its citizens. To counteract that, national cultural policy enters the picture again. Among the steps taken, the government's National Theater fosters the preservation of those forms deemed most important. (See my case study on Japan in this series.)

In time, governments around the world have established a variety of national cultural policies to meet the challenges posed by both internal heterogeneity and the forces of westernization. In Malaysia, the government's effort to promote national unity among a disparate ethnic population has resulted in the promotion of a newly created music that is based on traditional Malaysian music but incorporates Western influences (Chopyak 1987). The approach in China has been similar. In his volume in this series, Larry Witzleben discusses such nationwide institutions as the symphonicized Modern Chinese Orchestra and the music conservatory. On the other hand, he notes that regional and local musical styles are widely appreciated. Interchange, dialogue, even confrontations between those national institutions and local traditions have produced many of the new developments in Chinese music.

"Music nationalism" is the use of music specifically to assert the all-important sense of united community within a nation-state, and also to assert some sense of difference to citizens of other nation-states. The national anthem is the most obvious example of the powerful medium that music can be. Think of broadcasts you have seen of the Olympics and consider the sight of the gold medal winners, standing under their nation's flag, listening to their national anthem. That focused moment of music nationalism is meant to announce the winner with a musical signal, to set the victor apart from the other contestants, and also to engender a sense of pride among citizens of the medalist's nation.

Most new nation-states have a flag and an anthem; many of them also have an emblem. The emblem may be anything—something from nature such as an eagle, something material such as an airline, something cultural such as a musical instrument, or even a composer. Frédéric Chopin (1810–49) is a case in point: the great Polish composer (CD track 34) and pianist was successfully redefined by the Polish intelligentsia in terms of the changing contexts of Polish nationalism. Chopin had little experience of his country's folk music; rather, he was an international composer in the European tradition, stranded in Paris by political circumstances and personal choice. His late romantic style came to denote revolution and the struggle of the individual against the world. By the early twentieth century he had posthumously become a cult "Pole" in Paris, which, in turn, was part of what made him valued in Poland, a genius representing a distinctly Polish contribution to Europe's international culture. In socialist Poland, however, Chopin was celebrated for his adherence to his roots and his refusal to conform to the bourgeois aesthetics of romanticism. One way or another, he remained emblematic of the Polish nation.

One type of music that has been crucial historically in the construction of new nation-states is folk music. Its connection with nationalism and national identity is discussed below in the section on authenticity.

ACTIVITY 6.1 *Other than the national anthem, is there any music or musician that you consider to be emblematic of your nation? If so, articulate the reasons why that is, and how it or they are used.*

Other Groups. To segue from national identity to other types of group identity, I invoke the steelband, or pan (CD track 2, Figure 1.2) which was officially proclaimed the national instrument of Trinidad and Tobago. However, the emergence of the steelband as a national symbol draws us into stories of other types of identity—social class, ethnicity, race, gender (as told by Dudley in his case study in this series). An instrument of the lower class originally, pan began as an ingenious creation of poor people who made the most of meager resources; around 1940 people began to tune different pitches on the surface of metal containers such as paint cans. Untrained musicians took pride in mastering the musical language of the educated class. When, in the nationalist movement of the 1940s and 1950s, the collection and promotion of folk music and dance was considered important, some intellectuals in Trinidad held up the steelband as an example of "urban folk" creativity. Its cultural status gradually ascended, and middle-class youth began to play in bands; by the 1960s women even began to play. During the 1970s schools all over Trinidad began to include steelband in the curriculum. When the prime minister declared it the national instrument in 1992, some Trinidadians of East Indian descent protested that such a symbol favored the status of Afro-Trinidadian culture over Indo-Trinidadian culture. But proponents of pan countered that the steelbands had come to include people of diverse ethnicities and classes. Regardless, Trinidadians could claim to have developed the instrument entirely on their own, and furthermore, because it had achieved international recognition, it was an ideal emblem for a unified national community.

As the steelband example shows, when the population of a nation-state is ethnically heterogeneous (i.e., multicultural, as most are), the relations of power can be quite complex. Political and cultural hegemony—dominance by some constellation of multiple social forces—usually emerges, as in the examples of Anglo-American or, in the larger picture, Euro-American culture in North American countries, Han culture in China, and Anglo-Australian culture on that continent. Other groups literally become Others, minoritized and sometimes marginalized within the nation-state. For those Others, music can be used as a means of identity assertion, to create solidarity, to protest.

For Mexican Americans, mariachi music has been an important expression of identity—national identity in Mexico, and also ethnic identity in the United States (CD track 29). Emerging from its rural roots in several states of western Mexico, the music of mariachi ensembles was seized upon in the early twentieth century by Mexican media and officialdom as an important expression of Mexican national identity. Mariachis appear with campaigning politicians, as "folkloric" entertainment for tourists, and in government-sponsored representations of Mexico to the international community. Mariachi musicians, however, often are quick to express the disjuncture between being glorified by officials as a source of national identity and pride on the one hand and being neglected or victimized by class prejudice on the other. In the United States, the Mexican American movement beginning in the 1960s and the emergence of mariachi-in-schools programs heightened the reverence for mariachi music as a positive signifier of cultural identity. As discussed in Daniel Sheehy's volume in this series, Mexican-born mariachi musicians point to the respect and appreciation shown to them by American audiences, and thousands of young Mexican Americans enthusiastically have taken up mariachi music as a closely held badge of personal and group identity.

In the United States, the assertion of black ethnicity and African roots through music has been extremely effective sociopolitically. So effective, in fact, that some Americans of Asian descent have modeled their political musical activity on that of African Americans. Without a shared musical heritage, Japanese American and Chinese American musicians joined the world of jazz performance in the 1970s, thereby lifting that powerful African American musical voice in the assertion of their Asian American identity and rights. Influenced in the 1970s by the black power movement in the United States and Rastafarianism in Jamaica, black ethnicity became a major sociopolitical issue in Brazil. Music groups endorsed the ideology of the 1940s and 1950s that is still called "negritude;" their songs evoked their African ancestry and the "black is beautiful" theme, but also raised quite vehemently the questions of racism and its resulting socioeconomic injustices (Gerard Behague, personal communication, 2001).

AUTHENTICITY

The association of music with national, ethnic, and other types of identity gives rise to one issue that just does not go away. In fact, concern with it is due largely to nationalism. As observed by Peter Wade in his *Music, Race, and Nation* on music in Colombia:

> The notion of the modern homogeneous nation in Latin America owes a great deal to European models, not just for the structures of the nation-state, but for the basic cultural values of "civilization" espoused by elites. This has led to debates within Latin American political and intellectual elites about "imitation" and "authenticity": some nationalist currents have felt that a "proper" nation cannot simply be a copy of some other (notionally original) societies and cultures; there must be some authentic cultural traditions to create originality, difference, and hence identity. (2000: 11–12)

The linking of authenticity to music came about through the thinking of the Prussian preacher Johann Herder from the late eighteenth century. Herder argued as follows (as summarized in Taruskin 2001): Language makes humans human, but it must be learned socially, in a community. Since thought is based on language, human thought is a community product. Each language manifests unique values and ideas. When the concept of language was extended to learned behavior or expressive culture—customs, music, and so on—they too were seen as essential constituents of a precious collective spirit. Expression of the collective spirit became an explicit goal of the arts. Distinctive culture could serve both as a marker of difference in external relations and a symbol behind which the citizenry could rally as a community. Thus was born the concept of authenticity as faithfulness to one's essential nature.

Authenticity became a thing as well as a quality. Where was it to be found and in what forms? Herder placed authenticity with the folk: folklore was authentic wisdom, folk music the true music of a people. With folklore elevated in value, its appropriation by elite culture to express national identity began to flourish.

The ambitious collecting of items of folk expressive culture began (with Herder himself). The collecting of folk music—songs particularly, due to the value accorded to language—became an important activity of prominent figures in the history of ethnomusicology and of European music such as the Hungarian composers Béla Bartók (1881–1945) and Zoltán Kodály (1882–1967). Post–World War II socialist nations' collecting was and is state-sponsored, with the focus on archiving songs as items—the possessions of a nation, or of a region within a nation, or some other distinguishable group. Composers also collected in order to have new material for their creative work.

Questions of authenticity and folk music remained closely linked, and aspects of Herder's thinking resonated still in the publications of Maude Karpeles, an important figure in folk music research in the first half of the twentieth century. In the *Journal of the International Folk Music Council* in 1951, Karpeles defined authenticity in folk music: developing unconsciously, evolving through a process of continuity, variation, and selection, and transmitted orally. While the word "authenticity" does not appear, and her "developing unconsciously" became "springing from the creative impulse," Karpeles's hand can be seen in a resolution of the IFMC in 1953, in which folk music is defined as a "thing" that exists owing to certain creative processes:

> Folk music is the product of a musical tradition that has been evolved through the process of oral transmission. The factors that shape it are: (i) continuity which links the present to the past; (ii) variation which springs from the creative impulse of the individual or the group; and (iii) selection by the community, which determines the form or forms in which the music survives. (*Journal of the IFMC* 5 [1953]: 23)

Even very recently, where the words "authenticity" and "authentic" appear in writing about music, they are likely to refer to one or more elements in that definition of folk music. I shall focus on each of those elements in turn.

The idea of a product occurs twice in the IFMC definition: "Folk music is [a] product," and then "the form or forms in which the music survives." Whether one calls them "objects," "items," or "forms," "products" are thought of as possessing (or lacking) authenticity. In the flurry of 1980s research and argument about authentic performance practice of European music before 1750, for example, the aim was to perform as authentic an object (a piece of music) as possible—using period instruments or new instruments modeled after them, trying to learn from written sources how ornaments would have been produced, and the like.

In this way of thinking about authenticity, the act of performing also becomes an object (or, as Taruskin puts it, a text). It is happening, for instance, when, in the interest of "authentic performance," a conscientious conductor of a non-Bulgarian choral group works with the singers to achieve a sound as close as possible to that of a traditional Bulgarian chorus. Whereas the authenticity movement in musicology was a historical project, contemporary multicultural projects are more likely to try to produce "authentic performances" modeled after performance as it is heard in recent times.

Authenticity is also thought of as residing in a person who has acquired the knowledge that permits him or her to perform authentically or to evaluate "authenticity" as a critic. Here, "authenticity" resembles "authority." As Taruskin states it: "Authenticity . . . is knowing what you mean and whence comes that knowledge. And more than that, authenticity is knowing what you are, and acting in accordance with that knowledge" (1995: 56). Taruskin's "you" puts the emphasis on a person's individual identity. The matter of authenticity's residing in a person emerges for ethnomusicologists who seriously pursue the practice of a contemporary music as a means of doing research. A lively debate persists with regard to those persons' "authenticity" as performers if the music is not one they grew up knowing. Often the debate is about whether it is "really" possible to be bimusical or multimusical (equally "authentic" in more than one tradition of musical practice), or whether someone who is not native to a culture can possibly be an authentic culture bearer of the music of another culture—knowing something inside out, in a manner of speaking. The debate usually arises because some individuals consider themselves to be authoritative in a non-native musical practice, while others doubt the authenticity of that identity. You can pose the same question about performers of early European music who did not live at the time and therefore in the culture of the music they are performing.

ACTIVITY 6.2 *Discuss these questions with your friends: Do you think a non-native musician can be an "authentic" performer of Indian classical music? Can a Japanese musician be an "authentic" performer of jazz or European classical music? Can a white person be an "authentic" performer of black music? Can a black person be an "authentic" performer in the European operatic tradition?*

"Authenticity" becomes easily paired with the idea of "tradition" as in the IFMC definition: "Folk music is the product of a musical tradition." Even in this definition, however, "tradition" is difficult to define. It appears to be a style of performance, or a musical genre—something within which items evolve. David Coplan defines tradition as "dependent upon a symbolically constituted past whose horizons extend into the present" (1990: 40). For the purposes of this discussion, the key idea is that a tradition links the present with the past.

The nature of "the past" to which tradition is linked has been a subject of much discussion in the humanities in recent years. In her study of the American genre of country music, Joli Jensen found that enthusiasts locate "the past" in whatever they believe to be disappearing in modern life and find the expression of nostalgia in country music to be useful in facing the realities of the present:

> I believe that we ratify the conflicts of modernity by ascribing to country music the authenticity we see evaporating in the present. . . . Country music, and its burden of maintained authenticity, is a way to address, obliquely but intensely, unresolvable conflicts in modern life. . . . Various markers designate country music's "realness": natural origins, spontaneous production, communal performance, heartfelt lyrics, sincere performers, and loyal fans are among the aspects invoked to prove that country music is more real than other forms. (1998: 160–61)

"Natural origins [if she means creative impulse], spontaneous production, communal performance"—these phrases resonate with the ideas in the IFMC definition of folk music.

Nostalgia pervades the sense of the past of youth in Bulgaria, who conceive "traditional experiences" as those that precede modern experiences (see Rice's book on Bulgaria in this series). They yearn for music that does not use the most obvious devices of modern popular and classical music such as loud electronic instruments and percussion. I will return to other ideas about "the past" below.

Commercialization and the media are two realities of modern life that emerge in discussions of "authenticity." Often it is in the context of the consideration of change, or "variation," as it is put in the IFMC definition of folk music. That folk music changes is not at issue: change or variation is taken to be natural and is still generally accepted as part of the folk music process. It is the reason for the change that causes concern about authenticity. Karpeles argued in 1968 that "genuine folk song" is not possible in modern industrialized society ([10]), and that idea still lingers, with commercialization, mass media, and other characteristics of modern life being regarded as negative forces. Jensen comments on this, with respect to the audience for country music.

> When country music changed in the 1950s, many attacked the shift as commercialization. The fear was that country music, infected by outside forces like the media and big business, was becoming less authentic, less real, more commercial. This draws on claims of the mass culture debate and on metaphors evident in the production of culture perspective. It imagines music as representing and offering authenticity and imagines the media and the marketplace as outside forces—polluting, contaminating, inauthentic. (1998: 161)

Jensen herself, however, responds that country music has been fundamentally commercial in origin and purpose since at least the 1920s. In the language of cultural studies, the scholar of popular music Richard Middleton would likely denounce the reactions of Jensen's informants as bourgeois attempts to devalue urban industrial working-class culture, attempts rooted in a romantic critique of industrial society (or more generally modernity) (1990: 130, 168–69).

In fact, commercialization is part of the reality of a good deal of music that is considered to be "traditional." In his volume on Mexican and Mexican American music in this series, Dan Sheehy explores this with regard to mariachi music (CD track 29). Mariachi music is at once a music rooted in over 150 years of tradition, a commodity governed by market considerations, and a dynamic, evolving musical stream of activity. It is shaped and expanded by tributaries of musical innovation and social meaning from the American side of the border. According to Sheehy, a key to knowing mariachi music "from the inside out" is understanding mariachi musicians as a community linked by their common occupation.

The community, or group, is another element that obviously emerges in discussion of authenticity. It appears in the IFMC definition of folk music in two ways that resonate with Sheehy's remark about mariachi: the group as a source of musical creativity and an agent for selection of what will endure. Joli Jensen and many other scholars have looked at it from the opposite perspective: music constructing community, and musical change disrupting community.

> When a new genre's authenticity is challenged it is an acknowledgement that culture constructs social groups. In displacing the honky-tonk sound as the dominant kind of country music, the Nashville Sound abandoned, even betrayed, those fans who loved the sound of

steel and fiddle. Social groups—call them fans, audiences, markets, or communities—are constructed in and through cultural genre. Changes in the genre change the ways people in these groups can define themselves and their relationship to each other. (1998: 163)

Here, a musical genre is an "authentic" item, in that it is expected to adhere to a model on which there is consensus and bears meaning around which a group can form. This notion is familiar from discussion above of the process of community building in nation-states.

The roots of an idea called "authenticity," then, lie in the modern Western world and in cultural politics. Ideas about authenticity emerged in relation to folk culture, and even when they develop about something without that connection, they generally involve a link to tradition or at least to some idea about "the past." Notions of authenticity in music are generally held to be constructed: "Claims about authenticity . . . are involved in a power struggle over the ownership of value in which tradition and modernity are key terms" (Wade 2000: 25). While the sociologist George Lipsitz suggests that "concepts of cultural practice that privilege autonomous, 'authentic,' and non-commercial culture as the only path to emancipation do not reflect adequately the complexities of culture and commerce in the contemporary world" (1994:16), we still find notions of authenticity proclaimed, as people make music meaningful and useful in their lives.

ACTIVITY 6.3 *Can you identify some musical genre you think about in terms of "authenticity"? If so, articulate your ideas about what makes an item in that genre "authentic" or not. Then consider the points above, relative to your ideas.*

TRANSCENDING BOUNDARIES

Ethnomusicologists are now vitally interested in the transcendence of boundaries by both people and music. To end this chapter as I began it, I return to the topic of globalization, with its processes that transcend boundaries of various sorts—ethnic, gender, national, racial, class, stylistic, and others. Those processes cause musicians to challenge senses of ownership of cultural property and concepts of authenticity, and they foster hybridization and synthesis.

"Trans-" is the operative prefix, as in the process of transcending ethnic boundaries. In East Africa, for instance, where a number of ethnic groups with different value systems reside together, musical contexts provide important opportunities for negotiating differences. Negotiation takes the form of friendly competition, as popular entertainment events include musical performances such as song duels, choir competitions, drumming, and dance contests (see Barz's volume on East Africa in this series).

Gender boundaries in instrumental performance are being transcended by some individual musicians. Stella Chiweshe of Zimbabwe is the first woman to achieve acceptance and fame as an *mbira* performer, and in Bulgaria Maria Stoyanova has established a fine reputation on a male-gendered bagpipe, the *gaida*. In Mexican and Mexican American culture, shifting gender relations are inviting women to take a more active role in mariachi performance (CD track 29); whereas women were typically excluded from public performance except as singers, many are now taking up the instrumental genre.

"Trans-" is the operative prefix again in the noun "transculturation," which has been espoused by the ethnomusicologist Margaret Kartomi to replace the term "acculturation" (1981: 234). Kartomi defines "transculturation" as "a process of cultural transformation marked by the influx of new culture elements and the loss or alteration of existing ones." Originally proposed by the Cuban anthropologist Fernando Ortiz, the term "transculturation" was intended to avoid the connotation of political hegemony implied by the older term, but it does more than that. It causes us to reconsider the matter of culture contact in the process of musical change. The term neither specifies nor even implies a physical location where the cultural transformation occurs. No people are specified, as in the "groups of individuals" in the definition of "acculturation" above. No circumstance of transmission is specified, as in "sustained first-hand contact." What is more or less specified is a sense of time, suggested by that contested word "culture." "Culture" usually implies some kind of history, some kind of continuity, some kind of "tradition." With the exception of that last factor, the term "transculturation" would seem appropriate to cover the circumstances of globalization in music.

ACTIVITY 6.4 *Since place, people, and circumstances of "influx" are not specified, you might find the idea of "transcultur-*

ation" applicable to music that has been created within a dias-poric group. Focusing on such a music that you are familiar with—salsa, gospel, Asian American jazz, country-style polka, for instance—write a brief essay arguing for or against the utility of the term to guide exploration of a process of change.

The Mass Media. The nature of "culture contact" in the globalization process is to a large extent mediated; that is, music can be experienced by people all over the world without their ever having experienced the people who created or performed the music. Already powerful in the modernizing process from the nineteenth century forward, the mass media are a potent force in the lives of just about everyone on the planet.

Many scholars share the opinion that the mass media's effects on musical cultures are neither positive nor negative in themselves; the effects depend on the uses to which they are put and the responses they engender. In a thought-provoking introduction to *Ethnicity, Identity and Music,* Martin Stokes suggests that the control of media systems by states, through ownership of the technology and its ability to exclude rival systems through censorship, is a tool of social control that few authoritarian states have overlooked. But media are not a sure means of enacting social control. A consumer can turn off a radio or television set, or tune to some other station. The rapid changes in recording and sound reproduction technology in recent years have arguably democratized recording and listening, and consequently weakened the grip of state and music industry monopolies (Stokes 1994: 12).

The roles of the media are too numerous to write about here, so two examples must suffice. Media can certainly play a vital role in legitimizing a music. Mwesa Mapoma has reported that in contemporary Zambia change is expected within expressive culture, and the mass media foster both traditional music and new popular music that is being created, primarily by youth who are adapting Western instruments to traditional norms (1991). The recording industry especially has been an important and powerful agent in the process of defining ethnicities and classes. We need only think of "race records" in the early history of the commercial recording industry in the United States to remember that. New recording technologies no longer imply quite the same kind of dependence upon large companies, however, and local industries all over the world are fostering local musical productions. Ethnomusicologists are studying such developments.

Transnationalization. To call a musical practice "transnational" is to imply that it is taken up in multiple locations simultaneously. "The notion of globalization understood as transnationalization—taken often as a synonym for universalization, meaning Americanization for some, Japanization for others, and neo-colonialization for yet others—takes for granted the erasure of geopolitical boundaries and the transcendence of space through mass-mediated communication . . . instantly shifting population groups and their reconstituting of space relations in tandem with the intense trafficking of ideas and goods and the networking of people" (Guilbault: forthcoming).

As a result of such "intense trafficking of goods and ideas," say Scott and Hast in the Irish volume in this series, the folklorist's definition of "folk song" is an artificial construction of no particular importance to traditional singers themselves. Their repertoire includes music hall song, locally composed songs, country music, rock, rhythm and blues, rap, fusion styles, and others.

The "intense trafficking of goods and ideas" is a given in the popular music sphere, of course, sometimes with the original association with place being weakened or lost. At present drums from many places are circulating among percussionists, and the rubric as well as musical practice of "world percussion" and "world beat" appears to be diminishing the significance of their origins. Several drummers with whom I have spoken have no knowledge of the origin of some of the instruments they are playing or of the indigenous drumming practice for which those instruments were created. Does this not cause us to continue rethinking familiar frameworks—the concept of authenticity, for instance?

Worldwide integration through technology and market exchange is the hallmark of globalization, and we are beginning to understand that many, if not most, musics have emerged from processes of hybridization or fusion. In his *Subcultural Sounds: Micromusics of the West*, the ethnomusicologist Mark Slobin has commented on fusion while noting the diversity of styles in the music of the *klezmer* musician Andy Statman. A leading mandolinist in bluegrass/newgrass music in the 1970s, Statman helped to found a fledgling *klezmer* movement, "a drive by younger Jewish-American musicians of differing pasts and persuasions to forge a new 'ethnic' style based on their neglected 'Jewish' roots." In the next fifteen years Statman's music branched out past the older *klezmer* sound to include not only his old favorite, bluegrass, but beyond. He explained to a reporter from the *New York Times* that "the orchestra plays traditional Jewish European music, but we also flow freely into bits and pieces of what we like. . . . It's our own form of improvisation, and folk music and the bluegrass influence is right there"; Statman calls the result "Moroccan African Mongolian klezmer music" (12 April 1992). Slobin rejoins: "In figuring out this stance, remember that the 'traditional Jewish European music' itself was a blend of styles including Moldavian, Ukrainian, and shades of Balkan, all transformed in New York in the 1920s and 30s" (1993: x).

In addition to problematizing notions of authenticity, this intense trafficking challenges concepts of the ownership of "culture" (the right to intellectual property). Questions with far-reaching implications are being raised. Should you or should you not be able to download music from the Internet without worrying about who owns it? Should the composer of the national anthem of a new nation-state be paid royalties on the song, as one individual is presently asserting to his government? Should poorer, economically dependent nations be forced by the United States and other powerhouses in the entertainment industry to change their local copyright conventions to conform to international copyright conventions that clearly work to the advantage of the powerhouses (a process seen by scholars of popular music such as Jocelyne Guilbault as a new form of colonialism)?

As transnational corporations create integrated global markets, the importance of the nation-state and ethnic groupings as sources of identity and identification recedes somewhat. Individuals grow more cognizant of their multiple, shifting identities (multiple subjectivities) as they think in terms of their nationality as well as their ethnicity, their affiliation with others in a transnational diasporic "community" (Clifford 1994), or gender or religious affiliation or something else that supersedes localized boundaries. For ethnomusicologists, this has meant looking at the ways people are making music meaningful and useful as they situate themselves in a globally oriented world—transcending old boundaries with a sense of freedom or erecting new ones to gain some sense of control, as they explore multiple musical practices made available and visible through the media and make aesthetic choices for themselves.

The Local.   Yet "the local" endures, in several senses of the word. For some transnational music, the original place associations of the music remain intact, however widely the musical style circulates and is played with creatively. Tango is Argentinian no matter where it is found; Irish music is Irish, no matter where it is made or who makes it; mariachi played in Los Angeles is recognized by everyone to be Mexican. The cultural space each occupies is linked to, but no longer dependent on, place.

The term "translocal" has been useful for the ethnomusicologist Tom Turino as he suggests an analytical possibility for narrowing the often unrestricted use of the term "global." He reserves the term "global" to describe phenomena such as the contemporary system of nation-states that "literally or very nearly encompass the totality of the earth" (2000: 6). Turino uses the term "cosmopolitan" to refer to objects, ideas, and cultural positions that are widely diffused throughout the world and yet are specific only to certain portions of the populations within given countries. Through the lens of music of Zimbabwe, in East Africa, he sees cosmopolitanism as always localized and always shaped by and somewhat distinct in each locale. "Cosmopolitan cultural formations are therefore always simultaneously local and translocal, i.e., situated in many sites which are not necessarily in geographical proximity; rather, they are connected by different forms of media, contact, and interchanges"— what he calls "cosmopolitan loops" (2000: 7–8).

Whether global or cosmopolitan, global-local or local-translocal, musicians at the present time negotiate complex sets of relationships. The example of a Haitian group, Boukman Eksperyans, is given by the sociologist George Lipsitz in his important book *Dangerous Crossroads*:

> Ever since their recording debut in 1989, the members of Boukman Eksperyans have been making music rendering them both dangerous and endangered. . . . Their 1990 carnival song, "Ke'-m Pa Sote" ("My Heart Doesn't Leap, You don't Scare me") played a part in the popular revitalization of voudou, helping to spark [an insurgent movement]. By connecting the dance hall with the voudou temple, "Ke'-m Pa Sote" also united town dwellers and rural peasants in opposition to the corruption that permeates Haitian politics. . . . Through its music, Boukman Eksperyans inverted, subverted, and reappropriated for revolutionary ends the rituals and symbols long employed by the [Haitian paramilitary forces] to preserve tyrannical rule. By the same token, they attempted to use the commodity culture brought to Haiti over centuries by foreign investment and foreign invasion as a focal point of resistance to the exploitation and oppression perpetrated on the people by outside powers and the country's own comprador elite. . . . The same circuits of investment and commerce that

bring low-wage jobs to Haiti's factories and fields carry the music of Boukman Eksperyans to a wider world audience. The same connections between U.S. multinationals and Haitian poverty that insures a perpetual presence on the island by the American security state also makes the visibility of Boukman Eksperyans in the U.S.A. a strategic resource for the group as they try to criticize their government and still stay alive. (1994: 8–10)

Boukman Eksperyans make music meaningful and useful not only in their lives, but in the lives of many others for whom they sing.

ACTIVITY 6.5 *Explore just how "global" your "local" musical choices are by making a systematic inventory. Visit the largest CD store in your location and make a catalog of the types of music available for purchase. Tune in to every radio station you can receive. Investigate all the explicitly artistic channels available through your TV. (Leave aside the Internet for this one.) Then situate yourself with regard to those choices, thinking about the perspectives discussed in this chapter.*

I have focused here on only a few of the lively issues that unify the case studies in this Global Music Series. My approach has been to contextualize them, to put them in the broader perspective of the intellectual work of the field of ethnomusicology. I now direct you to those case studies, where you can see the issues addressed in a "local" context.

CHAPTER 7

Thinking about Fieldwork

∞

Study through fieldwork is a particular hallmark of ethnomusicology, and this chapter guides you in experiencing that for yourself. Basically, doing fieldwork is the process of learning about something directly from people. Fieldwork is a window through which to learn how people experience music and express culture.

Where is the field and what is the work? Historically, "the field" meant any place other than a library (where materials recorded in some form are the primary source). And because most ethnomusicologists worked someplace other than in their own culture, "the field" meant somewhere distant. In reality, however, "the field" encompasses the library as well, because the best way to start is to find what has already been reported on the subject. In the broadest and most pragmatic terms, the "field" is anywhere we can learn about a topic, including with our own family and friends. Our home communities offer abundant field locations.

The "work" in fieldwork has always meant any kind of activity that contributes to learning about music. Making music is often a part of fieldwork; you can learn much by being a participant observer. Perhaps more importantly, when we put ourselves in the position of being a student of music along with other music makers, our experience is one of sharing rather than staring, and our relationships become less distant. Attending performances, hunting for recordings—numerous activities can be part of fieldwork. Even casual conversation about music turns into "work" whenever we begin to think about it systematically rather than in random fashion and to keep a record of what we have learned. Another term for it at that point is "field research."

Learning from people can be fruitful and fun if three guiding principles are followed:

1. Keep focusing on the purpose of your project.

2. Remember that you are seeking to learn from others, not seeking to prove something you have already decided is the case.

3. Imagine yourself in the position of any person with whom you are consulting. What kinds of questions would you enjoy (or not enjoy) being asked, for instance? Here the "golden rule" really applies: treat others as you want them to treat you!

PICKING A PROJECT

WORD OF ADVICE: *For your project choose something you can easily manage to do. It does not need to be a complicated topic; it should be a straightforward starting point. A broad topic should be narrowed.*

A project can be almost anything. Thinking from the people point of view, a good place to start might be doing a life history, to learn about someone's musical experience and the meaning of music in his or her life. For instance:

- Is there a member of your family who loves music, with whom you have never talked about it? This might be a good way to get to know a grandparent or aunt or uncle better.
- What is the musical experience of someone you know from another culture?
- What has the experience of music of your classmates been, and how has it influenced the kinds of music they like? How does music fit into their lives, and why?

Thinking from the topical point of view, identify something having to do with music that you are really interested in and build a project around it. For example:

- If you play in a band or sing in a chorus, explore the history of the group: When and why was it founded? What sort of people have belonged to it, and Why? Who has supported it financially? Where has it performed? How does it fit into the general music scene in the area?

- If there is a kind of music you really love, learn if there is a local group that performs it and find out about "living that music" from the music makers' perspectives. One of my students studied the reasons why other students play in pickup bands.
- If you like instruments, look for an instrument maker or repairer in your vicinity and learn about them from that perspective. One of my students found a local luthier to interview and observe at work.
- If you are interested in another field of study, try a topic that combines it with music. One of my students investigated the correlation of abilities in math and music.
- Propose a hypothesis to test. One of my students hypothesized that studying to music helps improve concentration.

WORD OF ADVICE: *Dedicate a notebook or computer file or some other repository to this project right from this early stage.*

WORD OF ADVICE: *Keep a diary-like journal of all ideas and activities, with entries dated. Note even things you try that do not work, such as connecting with an informant.*

WORD OF ADVICE: *Make a list in your journal of several possible projects. Many things can happen, so you need a backup idea.*

PLANNING THE PROJECT

Once you have an idea for a project, you should plan how to carry it out. Asking yourself some questions is a good way to test the viability of your project—whether or not you can manage to do it. If it becomes clear that one project is not easily doable, repeat this questioning process for other projects on your list until you find the right one for your interests and circumstances.

What: What sorts of activities will I need to carry out to do this project? Will it be sufficient to interview persons, or will I need to attend performances as well, or just hang out?

Who: Who will I need to speak to—one person or several? If one, is that person likely to welcome my questions and have time for me? If several, how many and why? Do I want to ask the same questions of each one, or do I want to learn about something different from each one?

When: Will it be easy to arrange a time to see the people I need to see? Where is the flexibility in my schedule? Can I adjust to their schedule, since they are doing me a favor? If they can meet only at night, for instance, can I manage that? If hanging out or volunteering to help with something in return is important, how much time can I allow for that?

Where: Where will I need to go to carry out this project? If it is at some distance, how will I get there? How much time will it take to get there and back? How far is too far?

Cost: Is this going to cost something monetarily? Do I need to make toll calls to speak with people? Do I have to cross a toll bridge to get somewhere or pay mass transit fares? Do I need to purchase a hosting gift if I visit someone's home? Pay for tickets for a performance or two? Have equipment such as recorders and cameras and supplies for them?

DOING THE PROJECT

Sometimes the most time-consuming part of a project is establishing the contact with the person or persons you need to speak with. Figure out before you call just how you are going to introduce yourself. Be ready to say who you are and why you are calling (see guiding principle 1 above). Do not forget to keep a record of each call you make or message you write—even if you do not reach the person or get a response. Be persistent: do not give up after one call. On the other hand, if you try for two weeks and never connect, then you know you had probably better not count on meeting that person. And if the person really does not seem to want to meet with you, follow guiding principle 2 and graciously say, "Thank you for your time anyway."

WORD OF ADVICE: *Call or write or—even better—go to the research location now! Do not put it off. Begin making contacts even before you have taken some of the steps suggested below.*

Here is where "the field" is located in the library. Search for studies already published that might guide you in your project. If, for instance, you are going to do a life history, find some published life histories that are based on interviews to get the flavor of such research; jazz history offers many such accounts, for instance. If you are going to learn about a musical organization, find a published history of a musical organization and analyze what questions were asked in order to write that history. If you are going to interview someone from another culture, do some basic reading about that culture and listening to its music. You will learn much more if you build on something.

Creating a survey questionnaire is one way to conduct research; conducting an interview is another. Before you meet with anyone, make a tentative list of questions you will work into the conversation. Formulate questions so that you are not leading the respondent to an answer. Practice interview or survey questions on a friend. You may discover that they are too general, too detailed, too personal, unclear, or drawing answers that are not the sort you were looking for. Keep honing the questions as you do the research; you need good questions to get good answers.

Think ahead about how you are going to capture what you hear in a conversation. Will you want to ask the person if you can record the conversation? If so, get the machine, tape, and batteries ready (extra ones, too!). Will you want to make a visual record of some sort? If so, be ready. If you or the person you are meeting prefers it, be satisfied with paper and pen to jot down quick reminder notes. Take along supplies just in case.

For further guidance, a list is the best help.

- Reread this chapter periodically to keep you on track.
- Make a checklist of everything you need to take when you go to meet with someone.
- In all your relationships with people, imagine yourself in their places. Show sensitivity in your interactions. Act with others as you want them to act with you!

- When you are interviewing someone, listen carefully. Follow up on things they say, as well as asking your planned questions.
- Soon after meeting with someone, summarize in your journal the most important things you learned. Then write up your impressions of that person as an informant—were they knowledgeable, vague, helpful, reluctant, and so on—as a guide for using the information they gave you. Discerning whether a person is a relative "insider" or "outsider" can be helpful (but you must define what you mean by those two statuses). If you try to do your project on the Internet, you will not be able to do the same sort of evaluating of your source that you can do in person.
- Figure out some way to double-check information you receive— by asking a second person the same question or checking a newspaper article perhaps.
- Label and date your recordings. Be sure to get people's names right. Keep a list of them in your notebook.
- Keep a list of the photographs you take.
- Enjoy yourself.

FINISHING THE PROJECT

To finish your project, plan some kind of oral or written presentation. Your journal, summaries and further notes, tapes, photos, questionnaires, and double checks are your resources for this. Do not forget to articulate some sense of your experience, as well as the results of your study.

- Organize an oral presentation.
- Write a report or article that you might submit for publication. Sending a write-up to the people with whom you worked is a good and ethical thing to do.
- Create some kind of art: a long poem or series of poems, a song, a visual essay, a painting or a video, a theater piece.

In addition to having learned about something that interests you, by carrying out your fieldwork project you will have learned more about how people make music meaningful and useful in their lives. In addition, you have put yourself in a better position to evaluate the results of ethnomusicologists' field research. There is a world of it out there to explore.

Glossary of Musical Terms

∞

Acceleration Speeding up the pace of the basic beats.

Additive meter Rhythmic grouping with subgroups of irregular numbers of counts.

Aerophone Instrument whose primary sound-producing medium is vibrating air.

Aesthetics Artistic values.

Accompanist Person performing a supporting musical part.

Ālāp-joṛ-jhālā-gat North Indian instrumental form.

Alto Lower female voice; instrumental range below soprano.

Aural transmission Learning by hearing.

Bar In Western meter and notation, one metric group of beats (also called MEASURE).

Bass Lowest vocal or instrumental range.

Beat In rhythm, equal-length durations or long or short subgroup in some systems of rhythmic grouping; in pitch, periodic variations in loudness when two sound waves with different frequencies overlap.

Binary form Musical structure of two different sections (AB).

Bridge On a chordophone, a component that holds the string up from the main body of the instrument.

Cadence Musical term for an ending.

Call and response Generally, the juxtaposition of solo with group; more specifically, a musical repartee between parts.

Canon Strict imitative polyphony, with the identical melody appearing in each voice but at staggered intervals (*see* ROUND).

Changdan Rhythm patterns drummed or otherwise articulated in Korean music.

Chord   In tonal music, three or more pitches sounding together in a functional way; intervals stacked vertically.

Chord progression   A sequence of chords that structure the music.

Chorus   In musical structure, long refrain added to song verse; main section of a popular song.

Chromatic scale   Scale using all twelve Western pitches within an octave.

Classification   A category with clear criteria.

Clave   In Caribbean and Latin American music, a rhythmic pattern repeated without change as a rhythmic foundation for a musical selection.

Colotomic structure   Articulation of the metric grouping by one or more instruments in a Southeast Asian ensemble.

Composing   Creating music, whether in the mind or in writing, whether to be repeated in the same form or subject to variation.

Compound meter   Meter in which each beat consists of a subgroup of three counts/pulses.

Chordophone   Instrument whose primary sound-producing medium is a vibrating string.

Corrido   Mexican and Mexican American narrative song genre.

Consonance   From medieval European thought, intervals or chords that sound relatively stable and free of tension; generally, an aesthetically pleasing interval or chord.

Concertmaster/concertmistress   Leader of the violin section of a European orchestra who functions as assistant to the conductor.

Corpophone   One's body used as a musical instrument.

Culture (musical)   Ways in which people make music meaningful and useful in their lives.

Deceleration   Slowing down the pace of the basic beats.

Diatonic scale   Scale comprising some arrangement of half and whole steps.

Dissonance   From medieval European thought, intervals or chords that sound relatively tense and unstable; generally, a discordant interval or chord.

Dominant   In tonal music, the fifth pitch up from a tonic; root of a dominant chord (V).

Downbeat In Western meter, count 1.

Drone One or more pitches sounding persistently.

Dynamics The volume of sound.

Electronophone Instrument whose primary sound-producing medium is electricity.

Enharmonic pitches In tonal music, two names for the same pitch.

Ensemble Musical group.

Flat In notation, a sign indicating that the note to which it is attached is to be played or sung a half step lower.

Form The shape of a musical selection; structure.

Frequency (pitch) In acoustics, rate of vibration (cycles per second) in a string, column of air, or other sound-producing body.

Fret On a cordophone, a component under a string but not touching it that indicates pitch placement.

Functional harmony Chords as used in the Western tonal system.

Gagaku Japanese court music.

Gamelan Term for "ensemble" in Indonesian music.

Genre A type of music.

Groove The way ensemble musicians interact during performance.

Half step Interval of a MINOR SECOND.

Harmony Pitches heard together; in tonal music, system of functional chords.

Heptatonic Systematic set of seven pitches.

Heterogeneous ensemble sound Combining instruments with different timbres.

Heterophony "Different voices"; musical texture of one melody performed almost simultaneously and somewhat differently by multiple musicians.

Hocket *See* INTERLOCKING PARTS.

Homogeneous ensemble sound Combining instruments with similar timbres.

Homophony "Same voice"; musical texture of block chords, or melody with chords.

Idiomaticity   Musical material resulting partially from an instrument's capability.

Idiophone   Instrument whose primary sound-producing medium is the body of the instrument itself.

Imitative polyphony   Musical texture of one instrument or voice "imitating" the material of another part.

Improvisation   Result of a musician exercising relatively great flexibility with given material.

Instrumentation   Instruments used in a musical selection.

Interlocking parts   Texture of one musical part subdivided among several musicians; in a polyrhythmic texture, coordination among multiple musical parts.

Interval   Distance spanned between two pitches.

Intonation   Sense of pitch placement.

Jig   Irish dance genre in compound meter.

Key   In tonal music, a tonality named after the main pitch.

Leading tone   In tonal music, the pitch a half step above or below the tonic.

Major scale   Western scale with whole steps and half steps arranged W W H W W W H within an octave.

Major second   Western whole step; interval spanning two half steps.

Maqam (makam)   Term for melodic mode in Middle Eastern music.

Mariachi   Mexican genre for string and brass ensemble.

Measure   In Western meter and notation, one metric group of beats (also called BAR).

Melody   Any selection of pitches in succession. "A melody" is a particular succession of pitches, see motive, tune.

Membranophone   Instrument whose primary sound-producing medium is a vibrating skin.

Metallophone   Pitched metal percussion instrument.

Meter   Regular grouping of beats.

Metric cycle   Repeating articulation of a grouping of beats.

Microtone   Some interval smaller than a Western half step.

Minor second   Smallest interval in Western music; also called *half step*.

Melodic mode   Generally, pitch material for melody bearing particular expressive qualities; in Western music, one of several species of the diatonic scale.

Mnemonic   Formula (in music, usually syllable) to aid in memorizing.

Modulation   In a piece of tonal music, shifting from one tonal center to another.

Monophony   "One voice"; musical texture of a single melodic line and nothing else.

Motive   Melodic or rhythmic fragment used to construct a larger musical entity; THEME.

Muqaddima   Term for the introduction in Arab ensemble music.

Musician   A person who experiences music as a practice.

Nonmetrical rhythm   Not organized in regular rhythmic groupings.

Octave   In Western music, interval spanning eight pitches, the highest duplicating the pitch name of the lowest; generally, the distance between two pitches in which the frequency of the second pitch is twice that of the first.

Oral transmission   Teaching by speaking, singing, or playing.

"Oriental" scale   Nondiatonic scale with major, minor, and augmented seconds arranged in the pattern m A m M m A m.

Ostinato   Constantly recurring melodic, rhythmic, or harmonic motive.

Overtone series   Relationship of the constituent frequencies of a single pitch.

Parlando rubato   Nonmetrical rhythm.

Part-counterpart   Structure in which one part is responded to by one or more supporting parts.

Pentatonic   Systematic set of five pitches.

Perfect pitch   Exceptional aural memory for pitch intonation.

Phrase   Usually, melodic unit; a musical thought.

Pitch   The quality of "highness" or "lowness" of sound; a sound produced at a certain number of cycles per second.

Pitch area   Acceptable range of intonation for a pitch.

Pitch hierarchy   Some pitch(es) in a pitch set given more importance.

Pitch register   An area in a pitch range.

Polyphony   "Multiple voices"; musical texture of two or more melodic parts performed together.

Polyrhythm   Musical texture of multiple rhythmic patterns performed simultaneously.

Program music   Instrumental selection associated with a story or other extramusical idea.

Pulse   Equal-length durations.

Quarter tone   Interval half the size of the Western minor second; in Arab music, half-flat.

Qawwālīyā   North Indian or Pakistani singer of Muslim Sufi music.

Rāga   Term for melodic mode in India's music.

Rāgamālikā   In India's music, a performance practice of progressing from one *rāga* to another.

Range   A total span; the distance from the highest to the lowest pitch.

Recitative   Singing that imitates and emphasizes in both pitch and rhythm the natural flow of speech.

Refrain   Repeating text and melody added to a verse.

Rest   A momentary silence in music; in notation, a sign indicating momentary silence.

Rhythm   Any succession of durations. "A rhythm" is a particular succession of durations.

Rhythmic mode   Rhythmic grouping bearing particular expressive qualities.

Ritardando (or *ritard*, Italian)   Gradual slowing of the pace of the basic beats.

Round   Tune designed to be performed as a CANON.

Rubato   Ebb and flow in the pace of the basic beat.

Salsa   Popular Caribbean dance music genre.

Scale   Pitch set (and therefore intervals) presented in straight ascending or descending order.

Scat syllables   Vocables used by jazz singers.

Selection   A piece or performance.

Sharp   In musical notation, a sign indicating that the note it precedes is to be played a half step higher.

Solfège   Syllables used to name pitches; sometimes, mnemonic drum syllables.

Solo   Performance by one person; a musical part meant to stand out.

Sonata form   A tripartite musical structure of Viennese origin.

Soprano   Highest vocal or instrumental pitch range.

Speed   The rate of the basic beats.

Staff notation   Western system of notating music on a five-line staff.

Steelband   Trinidadian ensemble featuring tuned metal pans.

Strophic form   Structure consisting of an entire melody repeated.

Structure   Shape of a musical selection; form.

Style   The combination of qualities that create distinctiveness.

Subdominant   In tonal music, the fourth pitch up from a tonic; root of a subdominant chord (IV).

Syncopation   In terms of beat, stress between the beats, offbeat; in terms of meter, accenting a beat where stress is not expected.

Tablature   Type of notation that gives technical performing instructions.

Tāla   Term for India's system for organizing measured musical time.

Tempo   *See* SPEED.

Tenor   Higher pitch range of a male singer or instrumental pitch range below alto.

Texture   Musical relationships among ensemble parts.

Theka   A one-cycle-long stroking pattern by which drummers articulate a North Indian metric grouping.

Theme   The basic subject matter of a piece of music.

Through-composed   Structure in which musical content changes from beginning to end of a selection.

Timbre   Particular quality of sound; tone color.

Tonal center   Some pitch in a pitch set given most importance in melody; key note, fundamental, primary pitch, tonic.

Tonal music   The system organized around having a functional tonic.

Tone   *See* PITCH.

Tone cluster   A vertical set of pitches, without the functional implications of chords in the tonal system.

Tonic   A tonal center; in Western music, the fundamental pitch of a scale or key; root of a tonic chord (I).

Triad   In tonal music, a simultaneous sounding of pitches a third and a fifth above the root of a chord; generally, a simultaneous sound of three pitches.

Tune   A relatively singable, fairly short, complete melody.

Tuning   Pitch(es) to which an instrument is set.

Unison   All performing the same part.

Vocables   Song text syllables that are not linguistically meaningful.

Waltz   Dance in triple meter.

Whole step   Interval of a MAJOR SECOND.

References

∞

Anderson, Benedict. 1991. *Imagined Communities: Reflections on the Origin and Spread of Nationalism.* Rev. ed. London: Verso.

Baily, John. 1985. "Music Structure and Human Movement." In *Musical Structure and Cognition,* 237–58. London: Academic Press.

Baines, Anthony, and Klaus Wachsmann, trans. 1961. "Erich M. Von Hornbostel and Curt Sachs Classification of Musical Instruments." *Galpin Society Journal* 14(3):3–29.

Barth, Frederick, ed. 1969. *Ethnic Groups and Boundaries: The Social Organisation of Culture Difference.* London: Allen and Unwin.

Begay, Shirley M. 1983. *Kinaaldá: A Navajo Puberty Ceremony.* Rough Rock, Ariz.: Navajo Curriculum Center, Rough Rock Demonstration School.

Berliner, Paul. 1978. *The Soul of Mbira.* Berkeley and Los Angeles: University of California Press.

———. 1994. *Thinking in Jazz: The Infinite Art of Improvisation.* Chicago: University of Chicago Press.

Berrios-Miranda, Marisol. 1999. "The Significance of *Salsa* Music to National and Pan-Latino Identity." Ph.D. diss. University of California, Berkeley.

Blacking, John. 1955. "Eight Flute Tunes from Butembo, East Belgian Congo." *African Music* 1(2):24–52.

———. 1961. "Patterns of Nsenga *kalimba* music." *African Music* 2(4):3–20.

———. 1997. *How Musical is Man?* Seattle: University of Washington Press.

Bordieu, Pierre. 1977. *Outline of a Theory of Practice.* Cambridge: Cambridge University Press.

Brinner, Benjamin. 1995. *Knowing Music, Making Music.* Chicago: University of Chicago Press.

Buia, Carole. 2001. "Best of Both Worlds." *Time,* special issue, *Music Goes Global,* 158(14)(fall):10–12.

Certeau, M. de. 1984. *The Practice of Everyday Life.* Berkeley and Los Angeles: University of California Press.

Chopyak, James D. 1987. "The Role of Music in Mass Media, Public Education and the Formation of a Malaysian National Culture." *Ethnomusicology* 31(3)(fall):431–54.

Clifford, James. 1988. *Predicament of Culture: Twentieth Century Ethnography, Literature and Art.* Cambridge, Mass.: Harvard University Press.
———. 1994. "Diasporas." *Cultural Anthropology* 9(3):302–38.
Coplan, David. 1990. "Ethnomusicology and the Meaning of Tradition." In *Ethnomusicology and Modern Music History*, edited by Stephen Blum et al. 35–48. Urbana: University of Illinois Press.
"Criteria for Acculturation." 1961. In *Report of the Eighth Congress of the International Musicological Society*, 139–49. Kassel: Bärenreiter.
Danielson, Virginia. 1997. *The Voice of Egypt: Umm Kulthûm, Arabic Song, and Egyptian Society in the Twentieth Century.* Chicago: University of Chicago Press.
Farley, Christopher John. 2001. "Music Goes Global." *Time*, special issue, *Music Goes Global*, 158(14)(fall):4–7.
Frisbie, Charlotte J. 1967. *Kinaaldá: A Study of the Navajo Girl's Puberty Ceremony.* Middletown, Conn.: Wesleyan University Press.
Guilbault, Jocelyne. Forthcoming. "Globalization and Localism" in *Enciclopediadella Musica Einaudi*, Vol. 3. Torino: Einaudi.
Handler, Richard. 1986. "Authenticity." In *Anthropolgy Today* 2(1)(February):2–4.
Herrera-Sobek, Maria. 1993. *Northward Bound: The Mexican Immigrant Experience in Ballad and Song.* Bloomington: Indiana University Press.
Hesselink, Nathan. 1996. "*Changdan* Revisited: Korean Rhythmic Patterns in Theory and Contemporary Performance Practice." *Han'guk Umak Yongu* [*Studies in Korean Music*] 24:143–55.
Hobsbawm, Eric, and Terence Ranger, eds. 1983. *The Invention of Tradition.* Cambridge: Cambridge University Press.
Hornbostel, E. M. von. 1928. "African Negro Music." *Africa* 1:30–61.
Jameson, Fredric. 1991. *Postmodernism, or The Cultural Logic of Late Capitalism.* Durham, N.C.: Duke University Press.
Jensen, Joli. 1998. *Nashville Sound: Authenticity, Commercialization, and Country Music.* Nashville: Country Music Foundation Press and Vanderbilt University Press.
Johnson, Charlotte I. 1964. "Navajo Corn Grinding Songs." *Ethnomusicology* 8(2):101–20.
Karpeles, Maude. 1951. "Some Reflections on Authenticity in Folk Music." *Journal of the International Folk Music Council* 3:10–16.
———. 1968. "The Distinction between Folk and Popular Music." *Journal of the International Folk Music Council* 20:9–12.
Kartomi, Margaret J. 1981. "The Processes and Results of Musical Culture Contact: A Discussion of Terminology and Concepts." *Ethnomusicology* 25(2)(May):227–49.
———. 1990. *On Concepts and Classifications of Musical Instruments.* Chicago: University of Chicago Press.

Kingsbury, Henry. 1988. *Music, Talent, and Performance: A Conservatory Cultural System.* Philadelphia: Temple University Press.

Klaser, Rajna. 2001. "From an Imagined Paradise to an Imagined Nation: Interpreting *Sarki* as a Cultural Play." Ph.D. diss. University of California, Berkeley.

Koskoff, Ellen. 2001. *Music in Lubavitcher Life.* Urbana: University of Illinois Press.

Kubik, Gerhard. 1979. "Pattern Perception and Recognition in African Music." In *The Performing Arts,* edited by John Blacking and J. W. Kealiinohomoku, 221–49. The Hague: Mouton.

Lerdahl, Fred, and Ray Jackendoff. 1983. *A Generative Theory of Tonal Music.* Cambridge, Mass.: MIT Press.

Lewis, J. Lowell. 1992. *Ring of Liberation: Deceptive Discourse in Brazilian Capoeira.* Chicago: University of Chicago Press.

Lipsitz, George. 1994. *Dangerous Crossroads. Popular Music, Postmodernism and the Poetics of Place.* London: Verso.

Lui, Tsun-yuen. 1968. "A Short Guide to Ch'in." *Selected Reports* (UCLA) 1(2):179–204.

Mapoma, Mwesa Isaiah. 1991. "Traditional Music in Contemporary Zambia." *Tradition and Its Future in Music. Report of SIMS 1990 Osaka,* edited by Yosihiko Tokumaru et al., 347–50. Tokyo: Mita Press.

Middleton, Richard. 1990. *Studying popular music.* Milton Keynes, U.K.: Open University Press.

Monson, Ingrid. 1999. "Riffs, Repetition, and the Theories of Globalization." *Ethnomusicology* 43(1)(winter):31–65.

Nettl, Bruno. 1954. *North American Indian Musical Styles.* Philadelphia: American Folklore Society.

———. 1975. "The Western Impact on World Music: Africa and the American Indians." In *Contemporary Music and Music Cultures,* edited by Charles Hamm et al., 101–24. Englewood Cliffs, N.J.: Prentice Hall.

———. 1995. *Heartland Excursions: Ethnomusicological Reflections on Schools of Music.* Urbana: University of Illinois Press.

Nijenhuis, Emmie te. 1974. *Indian Music: History and Structure.* Leiden: E. J. Brill.

Nzewi, Meki. 1991. *Musical Practice and Creativity: An African Traditional Perspective.* Bayreuth: IWALEWA-Haus, University of Bayreuth.

Qureshi, Regula. 1987. "*Qawwali*: Making the Music Happen in the Sufi Assembly." *Asian Music* 18(2)(spring/summer):118–57.

"Resolution on the Definition of Folk Music." 1953. *Journal of the International Folk Music Council* 5:23.

Said, Edward. 1978. *Orientalism.* Harmondsworth, U.K.: Penguin.

Santosa. 2001. "Constructing Images in Gamelan Performances: Communicative Aspects among Musicians and Audiences in Village Communities." Ph. D. diss. University of California, Berkeley.

Slobin, Mark. 1993. *Subcultural Sounds: Micromusics of the West.* Hanover, N.H.: Wesleyan University Press and University Press of New England.

Small, Christopher. 1998. *Musicking: The Meanings of Performing and Listening.* Hanover, H.H.: Wesleyan University Press.

Stokes, Martin, ed. 1994. *Ethnicity, Identity and Music: The Musical Construction of Place.* Oxford: Berg.

Sugarman, Jane. 1997. *Engendering Song: Singing and Subjectivity at Prespa Albanian Weddings.* Chicago: University of Chicago Press.

Taruskin, Richard. 1995. *Text and Act: Essays on Music and Performance.* New York: Oxford University Press.

———. 2001. "Nationalism." In *The New Grove Dictionary of Music and Musicians,* 2d ed., edited by Stanley Sadie, 17:689–706. London: Macmillan.

Taylor, Tim. 1997. *Global Pop.* New York: Routledge.

Théberge, Paul. 1997. *Any Sound You Can Imagine: Making Music/Consuming Technology.* Hanover, N.H.: Wesleyan University Press.

Turino, Thomas. 1993. *Moving Away from Silence: Music of the Peruvian Altiplano and the Experience of Urban Migration.* Chicago: University of Chicago Press.

———. 2000. *Nationalists, Cosmopolitans, and Popular Music in Zimbabwe.* Chicago: University of Chicago Press.

Wade, Peter. 2000. *Music, Race, and Nation: Música Tropical in Colombia.* Chicago: University of Chicago Press.

Wilson, Olly. 1992. "The Heterogenous Sound Ideal in African-American Music." In *New Perspectives on Music: Essays in Honor of Eileen Southern,* edited by J. Wright, 327–38. Warren, Mich.: Harmonie Park.

Resources

Fieldwork Guide
A Manual for Documentation, Fieldwork and Preservation for Ethnomusicologists. 2001. Society for Ethnomusicology.

Reference Works
The Garland Encyclopedia of World Music. 1998–. Routledge.
The New Grove Dictionary of Music and Musicians. 2001. Macmillan.

Journals: General
Cultural Anthropology. 1986–. American Anthropological Association.
Dance Research Journal. 1968–. Committee on Research in Dance.
Ethnomusicology. 1953–. Society for Ethnomusicology. See "Current Publications: Bibliography, Discography, Films and Videos" section in every issue through vol. 44 (2000), thereafter at ⟨http://www.ethnomusicology.org⟩.
The Journal of American Folklore. 1888–. American Folklore Society.
The World of Music. 1957–. Bärenreiter.
Yearbook of Traditional Music. 1968–. International Council for Traditional Music.

Journals: Particular Musics
African Music. 1954–. African Music Society, South Africa.
Asian Music. 1969–. Society for Asian Music.
Black Music Research Journal. 1980–. Fisk University.
Black Perspective in Music. 1973–90. Foundation for Research in the Afro-American Creative Arts.
Center for Black Music Research Digest. 1988–. Columbia College.
Journal of the American Musicological Society. 1947–. American Musicological Society.
Latin American Music Review. 1980–. University of Texas Press.
Popular Music. 1981–. Cambridge University Press.
Popular Music and Society. 1971–. Bowling Green State University.

Journal of Popular Music Studies. 1993–. U.S. Branch of the International Association for the Study of Popular Music.

Audio and Visual Materials

For listing and reviews of sound recordings, videos, and films, see *Ethnomusicology.* Here only prominent series are listed.

Bernard Wilets Discovering Music Series. Los Angeles: Encyclopedia Britannica Educational Corporation.

Caribbean Eye: A UNESCO/Banyan Project. Trinidad and Tobago: Banyan Archives.

Flower Films. El Cerrito, Calif.

JVC Video Anthology of World Music and Dance. 30 vols. 1990–. Victor Company of Japan, distributed by Rounder Records.

JVC/Smithsonian Folkways Video Anthology of Music and Dance of the Americas. 13 vols. 1996–. Smithsonian Institution.

Roots of Rhythm. Cultural Research and Communication. Los Angeles: KCET.

The Survey of Korean Music: Video Program Set. Seoul, Korea: National Center for Korean Traditional Performing Arts.

University of California Extension, Center for Media and Independent Learning, Berkeley, Calif.

Recording Companies

American Folklife Center, Library of Congress.
Archives Internationale de Musique Populaire.
Bärenreiter Musicaphon.
Le Chant du Monde.
Electra/Nonesuch Explorer Series.
EMI-Australia.
EMI-Odeon.
Global Village Music.
Globe Style.
Harmonia Mundi.
Heritage.
Lyrichord Discs.
Music of the World.
Ocora/Radio France.
Rounder Records.
Shanachi Records.
Smithsonian Folkways.

Index

∞